Introduction

Qualifications covered

This book has been written specifically to cover the Unit 'Indirect Tax' which is mandatory for the following qualifications:

■ AAT Advanced Diploma in Accounting – Level 3

■ AAT Advanced Certificate in Bookkeeping – Level 3

■ AAT Advanced Diploma in Accounting at SCQF Level 6

This book contains Chapter Activities which provide extra practice material in addition to the activities included in the Osborne Books Tutorial text, and Practice Assessments to prepare the student for the computer based assessments. The latter are based directly on the structure, style and content of the sample assessment material provided by the AAT at www.aat.org.uk.

Suggested answers to the Chapter Activities and Practice Assessments are set out in this book.

Osborne Study and Revision Materials

The materials featured on the previous page are tailored to the needs of students studying this Unit and revising for the assessment. They include:

■ **Tutorials:** paperback books with practice activities

■ **Wise Guides:** pocket-sized spiral bound revision cards

■ **Student Zone:** access to Osborne Books online resources

■ **Osborne Books App:** Osborne Books ebooks for mobiles and tablets

Visit www.osbornebooks.co.uk for details of study and revision resources and access to online material.

Indirect tax

(Finance Act 2018)

Workbook

for assessments from January 2019

Jo Osborne

Published by Osborne Books Limited
Tel 01905 748071
Email books@osbornebooks.co.uk
Website www.osbornebooks.co.uk

Design by Laura Ingham

Printed by CPI Group (UK) Limited, Croydon, CR0 4YY, on environmentally friendly, acid-free paper from managed forests.

MIX
Paper from
responsible sources
FSC® C013604

British Library Cataloguing in Publication Data
A catalogue record for this book is available from the British Library

ISBN 978 1911198 376

Contents

Introduction

Also available from Osborne Books...

Tutorials

Clear, explanatory books written
precisely to the specifications

Wise Guides

Handy pocket-sized study and revision guides

Student Zone

Login to access your free ebooks and
interactive revision crosswords

Download **Osborne Books App** free from the App Store or Google Play Store
to view your ebooks online or offline on your mobile or tablet.

www.osbornebooks.co.uk

Chapter activities

1 Introduction to Value Added Tax

1.1 VAT paid by a customer on a purchase invoice is treated as which of the following in the supplier's VAT Return?

(a)	Income tax	
(b)	Input tax	
(c)	Output tax	
(d)	Sales tax	

1.2 Decide whether the statement below is true or false.

'VAT is a direct tax.'

TRUE / FALSE

1.3 A sales invoice for taxable supplies that includes standard rate VAT is being processed by a VAT registered business. What will be the effect of this invoice on the VAT due to be paid by this business to HM Revenue & Customs?

(a)	It will have no effect on the VAT payable by the business	
(b)	It will increase the amount of VAT due to be paid	
(c)	It will decrease the amount of VAT due to be paid	

1.4 A VAT registered business issues a credit note to one of its customers. The credit note is for £100 plus VAT at 20% and relates to an original invoice of £560 plus VAT at 20%. What will be the effect on the VAT due to be paid to HM Revenue & Customs?

(a) It will increase the VAT payable by £20	
(b) It will decrease the VAT payable by £20	
(c) It will increase the VAT payable by £112	
(d) It will decrease the VAT payable by £112	

1.5 A retailer buys goods from the manufacturer for £500 plus VAT of £100. It then sells them to a customer for £800 plus VAT of £160. How is the total VAT of £160 paid to HM Revenue & Customs?

(a) All £160 is paid over to HM Revenue & Customs by the customer	
(b) All £160 is paid over to HM Revenue & Customs by the retailer	
(c) The retailer pays £60 and the manufacturer pays £100 to HM Revenue & Customs	
(d) The manufacturer pays the whole £160 to HM Revenue & Customs	

1.6 An invoice that includes goods at reduced rate VAT means that the rate of VAT charged on these goods is which of the following?

(a) 0%	
(b) 5%	
(c) 17.5%	
(d) 20%	

1.7   Which of the following is a likely reason for a business to choose to voluntarily deregister for VAT?

(a) It only supplies standard-rated products	
(b) Whilst it previously supplied standard-rated products it now only supplies products that attract reduced rate VAT	
(c) The owner of the business is winding the business down prior to retiring	
(d) The business only supplies zero-rated products	

1.8   Which of the following businesses can **voluntarily** register for VAT?

(a) A business that only supplies products which are exempt from VAT	
(b) An individual who sells his/her own second hand clothing on ebay	
(c) A business that annually supplies standard-rated goods with a list price of £47,000 p.a.	
(d) A business that supplies exempt goods with a list price of £98,000	

1.9   A business that registers for VAT receives which of the following as proof that it has registered?

(a)	A VAT Return	
(b)	Certificate of registration	
(c)	Trading certificate	
(d)	VAT control account	

1.10   Complete the following statement.

'HMRC recommends that businesses keep their financial records for at least [   ] years.'

1.11   A business reached the VAT registration threshold three months ago but did not register for VAT. It is now required to pay HMRC £7,500 in respect of output tax that it did not charge during this three month period.

Decide whether the following statement is true or false.

'The business's customers must now reimburse the business for the output tax payable to HMRC.'

| TRUE / FALSE |

1.12   A professional accountant who is responsible for completing the business's VAT Return should ensure that he keeps himself fully up-to-date with current VAT regulations in order to comply with which of the following fundamental ethical principles?

(a) Confidentiality	
(b) Objectivity	
(c) Professional behaviour	
(d) Professional competence and due care	

1.13   The owner of the business that you work for has given you a receipt for £1,800 for carpet and fitting. He has asked you to process through the business's accounts and reclaim the VAT in the usual way. When you look at the invoice closely you notice that the carpet has been fitted at the owner's home.

Which of the following is the ethical approach to take in this situation?

(a)	Explain to the owner that as this is personal expenditure it is disallowed for VAT so the VAT cannot be reclaimed	
(b)	Immediately report the owner of the business to HMRC	

2   VAT and business documents

2.1   There are a number of items that must be included on a full VAT invoice.

From the list below tick all items that must be included on a full VAT invoice.

	Must be included on a full VAT invoice
Customer order number	
Invoice date	
Description of the goods or services supplied	
Customer's VAT number	
Seller's VAT number	
Customer name and address	
Seller's name and address	
Seller's required payment method	
Rate of prompt payment discount (if offered)	
VAT rates applied	
Amount excluding VAT	
Amount of VAT charged	

2.2 Reynolds Ltd is registered for VAT and supplies some goods that are standard-rated for VAT and some goods on which VAT is charged at reduced rate. The invoice for one of its customers includes items at both these rates of VAT.

Which of the following statements about the VAT invoice that Reynolds Ltd issues to this customer is true?

(a) The invoice should only show the total VAT charges	
(b) The invoice should show the standard rate VAT and the reduced rate VAT as separate amounts on the invoice	
(c) The invoice should show the standard rate VAT separately and include the reduced rate VAT in the Gross amount due	
(d) The invoice should show the reduced rate VAT separately and include the standard rate VAT in the Gross amount due	

2.3 'A business can issue a simplified invoice if the amount charged for the supply including VAT is £ [   ] or less.'

Complete the sentence above by inserting the correct figure.

2.4 A business makes mixed supplies to a customer as follows:

- standard-rated supplies of £100 plus VAT of £20

- exempt supplies of £97

Decide which of the following statements is correct in this situation.

(a) The business can issue a simplified invoice as the total supplies including VAT are less than £250	
(b) The business can issue a simplified invoice as the total supplies excluding VAT are less than £250	
(c) The business cannot issue a simplified invoice as the invoice includes exempt supplies	
(d) Simplified invoices cannot be issued if there are mixed supplies	

2.5   Which of the following statements are true about a pro-forma invoice?

Tick all statements that are true.

	True about a pro-forma invoice
Pro-forma invoices must show the supplier's VAT registration number	
Pro-forma invoices are normally used to collect payment from a customer prior to supplying the goods	
Pro-forma invoices can only be issued for amounts up to £250 including VAT	
A customer cannot use a pro-forma invoice to reclaim input tax	

2.6   Charles runs a lighting shop. He buys 16 lamps from the wholesaler for £27.50 each including VAT. How much VAT will be included on the invoice from the wholesaler?

(a)	£88	
(b)	£73.33	
(c)	£5.50	
(d)	£4.58	

2.7   Marina is preparing an invoice for a customer for standard-rated goods (standard rate is 20%). The customer is entitled to a 10% trade discount. The list price of the goods is £220. What is the total VAT to be shown on the invoice?

(a)	£44	
(b)	£39.60	
(c)	£36.66	
(d)	£33	

2.8   Dolby Ltd supplies standard-rated goods to a customer at a price of £1,500 excluding VAT. The terms of the sale are that the customer will receive a prompt payment discount of 8% if they pay within 10 days. The customer pays the invoice within 7 days.

How much output tax should Dolby Ltd include in its VAT account for this supply?

£ [   ]

2.9   The business that you work for receives an invoice for £271.68, which includes VAT at 20%. What is the net amount of the invoice, and the VAT included?

(a) Net invoice amount is £226.40 and the VAT included is £45.28	
(b) Net invoice amount is £217.35 and the VAT included is £54.33	
(c) Net invoice amount is £271.68 and the VAT included is £54.33	
(d) Net invoice amount is £271.68 and the VAT included is £45.28	

2.10   Malcolm is registered for VAT and issues an invoice for plumbing services with a standard price of £440. He offers a trade discount to regular customers. The total amount including VAT shown on the invoice to a regular customer is £475.20. What is the rate of discount that has been given?

(a)	7.4%	
(b)	8%	
(c)	10%	
(d)	12%	

2.11 Ezra is the proprietor of a VAT registered business. On 10 July he receives an order from a customer for standard VAT rated goods. He delivers the goods to the customer on 12 July and issues an invoice on 16 July. The customer pays the invoice on 24 July. What is the tax point for this invoice?

(a)	10 July	
(b)	12 July	
(c)	16 July	
(d)	24 July	

2.12 Enrique runs a VAT registered business. A new customer orders standard-rated goods with a list price of £5,000. Enrique issues a pro-forma invoice dated 29 September. Payment for the goods is received on 3 October and the goods are delivered to the customer on 5 October. Enrique issues a VAT invoice to the customer on 6 October.

What is the tax point for this invoice?

(a)	29 September	
(b)	3 October	
(c)	5 October	
(d)	6 October	

2.13 HMRC publishes a VAT fraction to calculate the VAT included in a total amount. When the VAT rate is 20% what is the VAT fraction?

(a)	1/6	
(b)	1/5	
(c)	2/3	
(d)	4/5	

3   Inputs and outputs and special schemes

3.1   Arnold runs a VAT registered business that sells a mix of zero-rated and standard-rated goods. Which of the following statements is true of Arnold's business?

(a) Arnold can reclaim all the input VAT charged to his business	
(b) The amount of input VAT that Arnold can reclaim will be subject to de minimis rules	
(c) Arnold can only claim back the input VAT that relates to the standard-rated goods that he sells	
(d) None of the input VAT can be reclaimed by Arnold's business	

3.2   A VAT registered business supplies only zero-rated goods. The majority of the business's inputs are standard-rated for VAT. Which of the following will be true of the VAT Returns made by this business?

(a) Most of the business's VAT Returns will result in an amount payable to HMRC	
(b) The business will rarely have to complete a VAT Return as it supplies only zero-rated goods and so never has to pay money to HMRC	
(c) The business will only have to complete a VAT Return if it starts to supply standard-rated goods	
(d) Most of the business's VAT Returns will result in a repayment from HMRC	

3.3 A business has made £160,000 of supplies in a VAT quarter. Out of this £40,000 were VATable supplies and the remainder was VAT exempt. What proportion of the residual input VAT can be claimed back on the business's VAT Return?

(a) 100%	
(b) 75%	
(c) 25%	
(d) 0%	

3.4 JRB & Co is a VAT registered business which only supplies standard-rated services. The finance assistant is preparing the VAT Return. He has a query over three invoices which all include VAT at 20%: £230 for staff entertaining, £450 for a laptop computer and £329 for client entertaining. What is the total input VAT that JRB & Co can claim for these invoices on its VAT Return?

(a) £93.16	
(b) £113.33	
(c) £129.83	
(d) £168.16	

3.5 Juno is a plumber who is registered for VAT. He has recently refitted his bathroom at his home and has taken goods out of the business with a list price of £300 but which actually cost him £270. Had he used them in his business he would have charged the customer £390 (all figures exclude VAT).

What is the total amount including VAT that Juno should treat as drawings?

(a) £468	
(b) £360	
(c) £324	
(d) None	

3.6   Decide whether the following statement is true or false.

'The VAT on the cost of client entertainment can be treated as an allowable input tax, whereas the VAT on staff entertainment can not.'

TRUE / FALSE

3.7   Albatross Ltd, a VAT registered business, bought a brand new company car four years ago for £20,000 plus VAT. The company correctly reclaimed the input VAT at the time the car was purchased. Albatross Ltd has agreed to sell the car to a private individual. Decide which of the following statements is true.

(a) Output VAT should be charged on the sale of the car as the input VAT on its purchase was reclaimed by Albatross Ltd	
(b) Output VAT should not be charged on the sale of the car as the individual is not VAT registered	
(c) Output VAT should not be charged on the sale of the car because it is more than three years old	
(d) Output VAT should not be charged on the sale of the car because the standard rate of VAT has changed in the last four years	

3.8   A business purchases fuel that will be used for both business and private motoring. The business does not wish to keep detailed records of business and private mileage. Complete the following statement.

'The business can reclaim all the VAT charged and then pay [   ] to HMRC which is based on the CO_2 emissions of the vehicle.'

3.9   Which of the following is the tax point for goods supplied to another business in the EU?

(a) The 15th of the final month of the VAT quarter in which the supply was made	
(b) The later of the date on which the customer receives the goods and the 15th of the month following the month of supply	
(c) The later of the date on the invoice covering the goods or the 15th of the month following the month of supply	
(d) The earlier of the date on the invoice covering the goods or the 15th of the month following the month of supply	

3.10 The following conditions apply to a business operating one of the special accounting schemes available in the UK:

- Annual taxable turnover of £800,000
- Payments are made to HMRC four times a year
- VAT Returns are submitted once a year

Which of the following schemes is being used?

(a) Flat rate scheme	
(b) Cash accounting scheme	
(c) Annual accounting scheme	

3.11 Andrew is registered for the flat rate VAT scheme and the flat rate for his business is 7.5%. In the last quarter the following sales and purchases were made:

Standard-rated sales (including VAT at 20%)	£26,088
Zero-rated sales	£4,944
Purchases (including VAT at 20%)	£11,240

What is the VAT payable by Andrew's business for the quarter?

(a)	£2,327.40	
(b)	£1,956.60	
(c)	£1,484.40	
(d)	£1,113.60	

3.12 Complete the following statement.

'A business can operate the cash accounting scheme in conjunction with the [   ] accounting scheme but not with the [   ] accounting scheme.'

3.13 Which of the following businesses would most benefit from registering for the cash accounting scheme?

(a) A business that is given 45 days credit by its suppliers but which receives payment from its customers in cash	
(b) A business that pays its suppliers in cash but allows its customers 60 days credit	
(c) A business that makes all its sales and purchases in cash	
(d) A business that makes all its sales and purchases on 30 days credit	

3.14 Comsten Ltd operates the annual accounting scheme and its best estimate of its VAT liability for the next year is £89,100. What is the business's payment on account schedule for this tax year?

(a) Three payments of £29,700 paid in months 4, 7 and 10	
(b) Four payments of £22,275 paid in months 3, 6, 9 and 12	
(c) Nine payments of £8,910 paid in months 4 to 12 with a balancing payment in month 14	
(d) Nine payments of £990 paid in months 4 to 12 with a balancing payment in month 13	

3.15 James is a self-employed writer who produces articles for educational websites and online publications. He does not have an office and works from home. His turnover is £91,100 excluding VAT and his costs of goods are £2,050 including VAT.

If James has registered for the flat rate scheme what rate of VAT must he use?

(a) 20%	
(b) 16.5%	
(c) 5%	
(d) 0%	

4 The VAT Return

4.1 Vernon has completed his VAT Return for the quarter ended 30 September. The figure in Box 3 is £45,324 and the figure in Box 4 is £52,796. This will result in which of the following?

(a) Vernon will have to pay HMRC £7,472	
(b) Vernon will reclaim £7,472 from HMRC	
(c) Vernon will have to pay HMRC £45,324	
(d) Vernon will reclaim £52,796 from HMRC	

4.2 All supplies made by a business are taxable at the reduced rate of VAT. The business offers a 5% trade discount and this quarter all the sales recorded in the sales day book have been made to trade customers. If the list price of sales for the quarter is £65,342.88 excluding VAT, how much output tax will be posted from the sales day book to the VAT control account?

(a) £13,068.57	
(b) £12,415.14	
(c) £3,267.14	
(d) £3,103.78	

4.3 Lanuka Ltd discovers a genuine error in its VAT records. An invoice dated 17 August 20-1 was issued to a customer showing output tax of £76.94, however, the figure should have been £769.40. The VAT Return for the quarter ended 31 December 20-1 shows output tax of £35,345.

What will be the final figure for output tax on Lanuka Ltd's VAT Return for the quarter ended 31 December 20-1?

£ [   ]

4.4 A business discovers that a net error has been made on its VAT Return. In which of the following circumstances will the business **not** be required to make a voluntary disclosure?

(a) The net error is £10,294 and the quarterly turnover is £485,450	
(b) The net error is £14,234 and the quarterly turnover is £300,000	
(c) The net error is £8,435 and the quarterly turnover is £83,200	
(d) The net error is £13,222 and the quarterly turnover is £1,200,000	

4.5 Rogers Ltd has completed its VAT Return for the current quarter, which correctly shows an amount of £27,451 payable to HMRC. Rogers Ltd made a payment of £22,948 to HMRC for the previous quarter. Unfortunately, this amount has been entered into the VAT control account on the wrong side.

What is the uncorrected balance currently shown on the VAT control account?

(a) An amount payable to HMRC of £50,399	
(b) An amount payable to HMRC of £73,347	
(c) An amount receivable from HMRC of £4,503	
(d) An amount receivable from HMRC of £50,399	

4.6 For each of the following items decide whether it will be a debit or a credit in a business's VAT control account.

Tick Debit or Credit for each item.

	Debit VAT Control Account	Credit VAT Control Account
VAT figure from the Purchases Day Book		
Bad debt relief		
VAT on Cash Sales		
VAT figure from the Sales Day Book		
VAT on items in the Petty Cash Book		

4.7 A business has discovered that a customer who owes £4,238.40 including standard rate VAT has gone into liquidation and it will not receive any of the money owed. The business has written off the debt in its accounts. How much bad debt relief can the business claim for this on its next VAT Return?

£ [   ]

4.8 Desmond has been chasing payment from one of his customers and is now convinced that the customer will never pay. He wishes to claim bad debt relief on the invoice. Decide which of the following is not an HMRC requirement for a valid claim for bad debt relief.

(a) The invoice must be more than six months overdue	
(b) The debt must have been written off in Desmond's accounts	
(c) The customer must have gone into liquidation	
(d) Desmond must have paid the VAT on the invoice to HMRC	

4.9 This question is about completing an online VAT Return for a business for the quarter ended 31 December 20-0.

The following accounts have been extracted from its ledgers:

Sales account

Date 20-0	Reference	Debit £	Date 20-0	Reference	Credit £
31/12	Balance c/d	456,511.10	01/10 -31/12	Sales day-book – UK sales	423,060.60
			01/10 -31/12	Sales day-book – exports	33,450.50
	Total	456,511.10		Total	456,511.10

Purchases account

Date 20-0	Reference	Debit £	Date 20-0	Reference	Credit £
01/10 -31/12	Purchases day-book – UK purchases	137,281.40	31/12	Balance c/d	167,845.40
01/10 -31/12	Purchases day-book – EU acquisitions	30,564.00			
	Total	167,845.40		Total	167,845.40

VAT account

Date 20-0	Reference	Debit £	Date 20-0	Reference	Credit £
01/10 -31/12	Purchases day-book – UK purchases	27,456.28	01/10 -31/12	Sales day-book – UK sales	84,612.12

You are told that the VAT on acquisitions is all standard-rated.

Complete boxes 1 to 9 of the VAT Return (on the next page) for the quarter ended 31 December 20-0.

Online VAT Return for period ended 31 December 20-0   £

VAT due in this period on sales and other outputs	**Box 1**	
VAT due in this period on acquisitions from other EC Member States	**Box 2**	
Total VAT due (the sum of boxes 1 and 2)	**Box 3**	
VAT reclaimed in the period on purchases and other inputs, including acquisitions from the EC	**Box 4**	
Net VAT to be paid to HMRC or reclaimed by you. (Difference between boxes 3 and 4.) (If Box 4 is greater than Box 3, use a minus sign.)	**Box 5**	
Total value of sales and all other outputs excluding any VAT. Include your box 8 figure. WHOLE POUNDS ONLY	**Box 6**	
Total value of purchases and all other inputs excluding any VAT. Include your box 9 figure. WHOLE POUNDS ONLY	**Box 7**	
Total value of all supplies of goods and related costs, excluding any VAT, to other EC Member States. WHOLE POUNDS ONLY	**Box 8**	
Total value of all acquisitions of goods and related costs, excluding any VAT from other EC Member States. WHOLE POUNDS ONLY	**Box 9**	

4.10 This question is about preparing figures for a business's VAT Return for the quarter ended 30 September 20-0.

The standard rate of VAT is 20%.

The following accounts have been extracted from the ledgers:

Sales account

Date 20-0	Reference	Debit £	Date 20-0	Reference	Credit £
30/09	Balance c/d	401,370.00	01/07 – 30/09	Sales day-book – UK sales	248,950.00
			01/07 – 30/09	Sales day-book – exports	56,000.00
			01/07 – 30/09	Cash-book – UK sales	96,420.00
	Total	401,370.00		Total	401,370.00

Purchases account

Date 20-0	Reference	Debit £	Date 20-0	Reference	Credit £
01/07 -30/09	Purchases day-book – UK purchases	145,654.00	30/09	Balance c/d	167,854.00
01/07 -30/09	Purchases day-book – zero-rated imports	22,200.00			
	Total	167,854.00		Total	167,854.00

VAT account

Date 20-0	Reference	Debit £	Date 20-0	Reference	Credit £
01/07 -30/09	Purchases day-book – UK purchases	29,130.80	01/07 -30/09	Sales day-book – UK sales	49,790.00
			01/07 -30/09	Cash-book – UK sales	19,284.00

You are told that bad debt relief on a sales invoice for £948.75 excluding VAT is to be claimed in this quarter.

(a) Calculate the figure to be claimed as bad debt relief on the VAT Return.

£ [   ]

(b) Calculate the figure for Box 1 of the VAT Return – VAT due on sales and other outputs.

£ [   ]

(c) Calculate the figure for Box 4 of the VAT Return – VAT reclaimed on purchases and other inputs, including acquisitions from the EC.

£ [   ]

4.11 This question is about completing an online VAT Return for a business for the quarter ended 31 March 20-0.

The following accounts have been extracted from its ledgers:

Sales account

Date 20-0	Reference	Debit £	Date 20-0	Reference	Credit £
31/03	Balance c/d	410,294.10	01/01 -31/03	Sales day-book – UK sales	354,144.10
			01/01 -31/03	Sales day-book – EU sales	56,150.00
	Total	410,294.10		Total	410,294.10

Purchases account

Date 20-0	Reference	Debit £	Date 20-0	Reference	Credit £
01/01 -31/03	Purchases day-book – UK purchases	197,845.20	31/03	Balance c/d	198,969.40
01/01 -31/03	Petty cash – cash purchases	1,124.20			
	Total	198,969.40		Total	198,969.40

VAT account

Date 20-0	Reference	Debit £	Date 20-0	Reference	Credit £
01/01 -31/03	Purchases day-book – UK purchases	39,569.04	01/01 -31/03	Sales day-book – UK sales	70,828.82
01/01 -31/03	Petty cash – cash purchases	224.84			

You are told that in the last VAT Return the amount of input tax claimed has been understated by £167.00. You have been asked to adjust for this error.

You have also been told that bad debt relief of £117.00 can be claimed in this VAT Return.

Complete boxes 1 to 9 of the VAT Return for the quarter ended 31 March 20-0.

Online VAT Return for period ended 31 March 20-0		£
VAT due in this period on sales and other outputs	**Box 1**	
VAT due in this period on acquisitions from other EC Member States	**Box 2**	
Total VAT due (the sum of boxes 1 and 2)	**Box 3**	
VAT reclaimed in the period on purchases and other inputs, including acquisitions from the EC	**Box 4**	
Net VAT to be paid to HMRC or reclaimed by you. (Difference between boxes 3 and 4.) (If Box 4 is greater than Box 3, use a minus sign.)	**Box 5**	
Total value of sales and all other outputs excluding any VAT. Include your box 8 figure. WHOLE POUNDS ONLY	**Box 6**	
Total value of purchases and all other inputs excluding any VAT. Include your box 9 figure. WHOLE POUNDS ONLY	**Box 7**	
Total value of all supplies of goods and related costs, excluding any VAT, to other EC Member States. WHOLE POUNDS ONLY	**Box 8**	
Total value of all acquisitions of goods and related costs, excluding any VAT from other EC Member States. WHOLE POUNDS ONLY	**Box 9**	

4.12 Decide whether the following sentence is true or false.

'A business has submitted its VAT Return late for the first time. In this situation the business will be subject to a default surcharge.

TRUE / FALSE

5 VAT communications

5.1 A colleague who you work with in a VAT registered business tells you that she needs to contact HMRC about a VAT matter. She asks you what she should do in this situation. Decide in which order she should take each of the following actions by ranking them 1st, 2nd or 3rd.

	Ranking
Write to HMRC	
Telephone the HMRC helpline	
Visit the HMRC website	

5.2 Decide whether the following statement is true or false.

'If you submit your VAT Return online then you are only permitted to communicate with HMRC via email.'

TRUE / FALSE

5.3 You are the Accounts Assistant at a business and have just completed the VAT Return for the quarter ended 30 November 20-0. You have been asked by your supervisor to send the Finance Director an email advising her of the date by which the online quarterly VAT Return must be filed, the amount that the business needs to pay or reclaim and the date on which it is due for payment.

The figure in Box 5 of the return is £8,453.19 and represents an amount that is due to HMRC.

Complete the following email by filling in the gaps.

To	
From	
Date	12 December 20-0
Subject	Completed VAT Return

Please be advised that I have just completed the VAT Return for the quarter

ended

The VAT Return must be filed by

The amount of VAT payable/receivable (delete as appropriate) will be £

5.4 You are an Accounting Technician who works for a chain of clothing shops and you report to the Chief Finance Officer. You have been asked to advise him on how an increase in the rate of VAT would affect the business and what action would have to be taken as a consequence.

Today's date is 15 October.

Prepare a draft email to the chief finance officer providing information about some of the potential effects and consequences of a change. Choose **ONE** option to complete each sentence.

To: **(Accounting technician/Chief finance officer)**

From: **(Accounting technician/Chief finance officer)**

Date: 15 October

When the rate of VAT changes the business must consider whether the prices it charges to customers will change. These prices **cannot change until the date of the next VAT Return / must change on the date of the VAT change / can remain unchanged if the business chooses**.

The new rate of VAT must be reflected in the amount of VAT paid to HMRC **only if we change the prices to customers / whether we change the prices to customers or not / only if customers choose to pay the new prices**.

If the date of the VAT change falls during one of our VAT periods, our system must **apply a single rate of VAT during that VAT period / apply dual rates of VAT during that VAT period depending on the customer / apply dual rates of VAT during that VAT period depending on each sale transaction's tax point**.

Kind regards

A Technician

Answers to chapter activities

1 Introduction to Value Added Tax

1.1 (c) Output tax

1.2 FALSE

1.3 (b) It will increase the amount of VAT due to be paid

1.4 (b) It will decrease the VAT payable by £20

1.5 (c) The retailer pays £60 and the manufacturer pays £100 to HM Revenue & Customs

1.6 (b) 5%

1.7 (c) The owner of the business is winding the business down prior to retiring

1.8 (c) A business that annually supplies standard-rated goods with a list price of £47,000 p.a.

1.9 (b) Certificate of registration

1.10 'HMRC recommends that businesses keep their financial records for at least **six** years.'

1.11 FALSE

1.12 (d) Professional competence and due care

1.13 (a) Explain to the owner that as this is personal expenditure it is disallowed for VAT so the VAT cannot be reclaimed

2 VAT and business documents

2.1

	Must be included on a full VAT invoice
Customer order number	
Invoice date	✔
Description of the goods or services supplied	✔
Customer's VAT number	
Seller's VAT number	✔
Customer name and address	✔
Seller's name and address	✔
Seller's required payment method	
Rate of prompt payment discount (if offered)	✔
VAT rates applied	✔
Amount excluding VAT	✔
Amount of VAT charged	✔

2.2   (b)   The invoice should show the standard rate VAT and the reduced rate VAT as separate amounts on the invoice

2.3   'A business can issue a simplified invoice if the amount charged for the supply including VAT is **£250** or less.'

2.4   (c)   The business cannot issue a simplified invoice as the invoice includes exempt supplies

2.5

	True about a pro-forma invoice
Pro-forma invoices must show the supplier's VAT registration number	✔
Pro-forma invoices are normally used to collect payment from a customer prior to supplying the goods	✔
Pro-forma invoices can only be issued for amounts up to £250 including VAT	
A customer cannot use a pro-forma invoice to reclaim input tax	✔

2.6   (b)   £73.33

2.7   (b)   £39.60

2.8   £276   *Workings:* £1,500 x 92% x 20%

2.9   (a)   Net invoice amount is £226.40 and the VAT included is £45.28

2.10   (c)   10%

   Workings: £475.20 ÷ 120% = £396

   £440 – £396 = £44 discount

   (£44 ÷ £440) x 100% = 10%

2.11   (c)   16 July

2.12   (b)   3 October

2.13   (a)   1/6

3 Inputs and outputs and special schemes

3.1 (a) Arnold can reclaim all the input VAT charged to his business

3.2 (d) Most of the business's VAT Returns will result in a repayment from HMRC

3.3 (c) 25%

3.4 (b) £113.33

3.5 (c) £324

3.6 FALSE

3.7 (a) Output VAT should be charged on the sale of the car as the input VAT on its purchase was reclaimed by Albatross Ltd

3.8 'The business can reclaim all the VAT charged and then pay **fuel scale charge** to HMRC which is based on the CO_2 emissions of the vehicle.'

3.9 (d) The earlier of the date on the invoice covering the goods or the 15th of the month following the month of supply

3.10 (c) Annual accounting scheme

3.11 (a) £2,327.40

3.12 'A business can operate the cash accounting scheme in conjunction with the **annual** accounting scheme but not with the **flat rate** accounting scheme.'

3.13 (b) A business that pays its suppliers in cash but allows its customers 60 days credit

3.14 (c) Nine payments of £8,910 paid in months 4 to 12 with a balancing payment in month 14

3.15 (b) 16.5%

4   The VAT Return

4.1   (b)   Vernon will reclaim £7,472 from HMRC

4.2   (d)   £3,103.78

4.3   £36,037.46

4.4   (c)   The net error is £8,435 and the quarterly turnover is £83,200

4.5   (b)   An amount payable to HMRC of £73,347

4.6

	Debit VAT control account	Credit VAT control account
VAT figure from the Purchases Day Book	✔	
Bad debt relief	✔	
VAT on Cash Sales		✔
VAT figure from the Sales Day Book		✔
VAT on items in the Petty Cash Book	✔	

4.7   £706.40

4.8   (c)   The customer must have gone into liquidation

4.9

Online VAT Return for period ended 31 December 20-0		£
VAT due in this period on sales and other outputs	Box 1	84612.12
VAT due in this period on acquisitions from other EC Member States	Box 2	6112.80
Total VAT due (the sum of boxes 1 and 2)	Box 3	90724.92
VAT reclaimed in the period on purchases and other inputs, including acquisitions from the EC	Box 4	33569.08
Net VAT to be paid to HMRC or reclaimed by you. (Difference between boxes 3 and 4.) (If Box 4 is greater than Box 3, use a minus sign.)	Box 5	57155.84
Total value of sales and all other outputs excluding any VAT. Include your box 8 figure. WHOLE POUNDS ONLY	Box 6	456511
Total value of purchases and all other inputs excluding any VAT. Include your box 9 figure. WHOLE POUNDS ONLY	Box 7	167845
Total value of all supplies of goods and related costs, excluding any VAT, to other EC Member States. WHOLE POUNDS ONLY	Box 8	0
Total value of all acquisitions of goods and related costs, excluding any VAT from other EC Member States. WHOLE POUNDS ONLY	Box 9	30564

4.10 **(a)** £189.75

(b) £69,074

(c) £29,320.55

4.11

Online VAT Return for period ended 31 March 20-0		£
VAT due in this period on sales and other outputs	Box 1	70828.82
VAT due in this period on acquisitions from other EC Member States	Box 2	0.00
Total VAT due (the sum of boxes 1 and 2)	Box 3	70828.82
VAT reclaimed in the period on purchases and other inputs, including acquisitions from the EC	Box 4	40077.88
Net VAT to be paid to HMRC or reclaimed by you. (Difference between boxes 3 and 4.) (If Box 4 is greater than Box 3, use a minus sign.)	Box 5	30750.94
Total value of sales and all other outputs excluding any VAT. Include your box 8 figure. WHOLE POUNDS ONLY	Box 6	410294
Total value of purchases and all other inputs excluding any VAT. Include your box 9 figure. WHOLE POUNDS ONLY	Box 7	198969
Total value of all supplies of goods and related costs, excluding any VAT, to other EC Member States. WHOLE POUNDS ONLY	Box 8	56150
Total value of all acquisitions of goods and related costs, excluding any VAT from other EC Member States. WHOLE POUNDS ONLY	Box 9	0

4.12   FALSE

5 VAT communications

5.1

	Ranking
Write to HMRC	3
Telephone the HMRC helpline	2
Visit the HMRC website	1

5.2 FALSE

5.3

To	**Finance Director**
From	**Accounts Assistant**
Date	12 December 20-0
Subject	Completed VAT Return

Please be advised that I have just completed the VAT Return for the quarter ended **30 November 20-0**

The VAT Return must be filed by **7 January 20-1**

The amount of VAT **payable** will be **£8,453.19**

5.4

To: **Chief finance officer**

From: **Accounting technician**

Date: 15 October

When the rate of VAT changes the business must consider whether the prices it charges to customers will change. These prices **can remain unchanged if the business chooses**.

The new rate of VAT must be reflected in the amount of VAT paid to HMRC **whether we change the prices to customers or not**.

If the date of the VAT change falls during one of our VAT periods, our system must **apply dual rates of VAT during that VAT period depending on each sale transaction's tax point**.

Kind regards

A Technician

Practice assessment 1

Task 1

(a)   During the year a business supplies goods that are a mixture of exempt, zero-rated and standard-rated. Over the next 12 months the business expects the split to be £25,000 exempt supplies, £30,000 zero-rated supplies and £38,000 standard-rated supplies.

Which of the following statements is TRUE? Choose **one** answer.

(a) The business will not have to register for VAT in the next year but can do so voluntarily	
(b) The business will not be eligible to register for VAT at any point in the next year	
(c) The business will be required to register for VAT at some point in the next year	

(b)   Albert is completing his VAT Return for the quarter ended 30 September 20-0. He has a query about whether he can claim the VAT back on a purchase he has made and wishes to contact HMRC. He has asked you how he should proceed.

Rank the following courses of action that Albert should take in the appropriate order ie 1st, 2nd and 3rd.

	Ranking
Telephone the HMRC helpline	
Write to HMRC	
Search on the HMRC website	

(c)   Complete the following statement by selecting **one** option.

A business with a short period of trading that temporarily takes it above the VAT registration threshold is permitted to remain unregistered provided it can prove that its turnover will fall below the threshold…

(a) … almost immediately	
(b) … within the next six months	
(c) … within the next 12 months	

Task 2

(a) A business that is registered for VAT is supplying goods to a customer that is standard-rated. The amount charged excluding VAT is £224.

Is the following statement true or false?

'The business may issue a simplified invoice.'

TRUE / FALSE

(b) A business that is registered for VAT in the UK receives a credit note from one of its EU suppliers which is also VAT registered.

What will be the effect on the VAT Return for the UK business? Choose **one** answer.

(a)	Both input tax and output tax will increase	
(b)	Both input tax and output tax will decrease	
(c)	Input tax will decrease and output tax will remain the same	
(d)	Input tax will increase and output tax will remain the same	

(c) The following information is available about an invoice issued by a business registered for VAT in the UK.

· A customer places an order with the business on 25 January and includes a 25% deposit with the order

· The business issues a VAT invoice for the deposit on 26 January

· The goods are delivered to the customer on 28 January together with an invoice for the remaining 75%

· The customer pays the invoice for the remaining 75% on 1 February

For VAT purposes what is/are the tax point(s) for this transaction?

Choose **one** answer.

(a)	The tax point for the deposit is 25 January and for the balance is 28 January	
(b)	The tax point for the deposit is 26 January and for the balance is 1 February	
(c)	The tax point for the deposit and the balance is 26 January	
(d)	The tax point for the deposit and the balance is 28 January	

(d) A business despatches goods to a customer on 19 August. What is the latest date that the business is permitted to issue a VAT invoice?

(e)   A business makes standard-rated, zero-rated and exempt supplies. Decide which of the following statements is true regarding the business's input tax for the period.

Choose **one** answer.

(a) If the exempt supplies exceed the 'de minimis' limit all of the input tax can be reclaimed	
(b) If the zero-rated supplies exceed the 'de minimis' limit all of the input tax can be reclaimed	
(c) If the exempt supplies are below the 'de minimis' limit all of the input tax can be reclaimed	
(d) If the zero-rated supplies are below the 'de minimis' limit all of the input tax can be reclaimed	

Task 3

(a)   The following conditions apply to a business operating a single special accounting scheme for VAT.

- The business has an annual taxable turnover of £920,000

- The business makes three interim payments each of 25% of the estimated VAT liability for the year

- The business submits one VAT Return for the year

Which of the following schemes is being used by the business? Choose **one** answer.

(a) Flat rate scheme	
(b) Cash accounting scheme	
(c) Annual accounting scheme	

(b)   A VAT registered business is expected to submit its VAT Return and any VAT payable by the due date.

Which of the following is the consequence for a business that fails to submit its VAT Return on the due date? Choose **one** answer.

(a) If this is the first time the business has made a late submission the business will only be required to pay a surcharge if it further defaults in the following 12 months	
(b) The business will be required to pay a surcharge because of the late submission	
(c) Provided no VAT is due to HMRC the business will not have to pay a surcharge	

(c)   A business does not currently operate any of the special accounting schemes. It wrote off an invoice on 12 September that was originally issued on 3 May. The invoice amount was £2,340 including VAT at standard rate. All the necessary conditions for claiming bad debt relief have been met by the business.

(1)   How much bad debt relief can be claimed by the business?

£ [   ]

(2)   What is the earliest opportunity for the business to claim bad debt relief on this invoice? Choose **one** answer.

(a) In its VAT period ending 28 February	
(b) In its VAT period ending 31 May	
(c) In its VAT period ending 31 August	
(d) In its VAT period ending 30 November	

Task 4

(a)   The Accounts Assistant at Desbel Ltd has discovered the following genuine error in the business's accounting records. An invoice received from a supplier which was recorded in Desbel's accounts in April 20-0 shows input tax of £472.30 when the figure should have been £47.23.

The VAT Return for the quarter ended 30 September 20-0 shows input tax of £7,433.00.

What will be the final figure for the input tax on the VAT Return for the quarter ended 30 September 20-0?

£ [   ]

(b)   The Box 6 figure on the current VAT Return of a large business is £2,333,400. The accountant has discovered a net error in its previous VAT period of £26,220. The business has corrected this net error on its current VAT Return but has not separately notified HMRC of the error. What will be the consequence of this for the business?

Choose **one** option.

(a) HMRC will view this as the incorrect action to have been taken and will issue a surcharge liability notice	
(b) HMRC will view this as a deliberate error and issue a penalty	
(c) HMRC will view this as the correct action and there will be no further consequences for the business	

(c)   A business submitted its VAT Return a month late due to its accountant being on maternity leave. This is the first time the business has submitted its VAT Return late. In this situation the business will be subject to a default surcharge.

TRUE/FALSE

(d)   **(1)**   A business bought a new company van four years ago. At the time of purchase the business correctly claimed the input VAT on the van. The business is now going to sell the van to a self-employed plumber who is not registered for VAT.

Which of the following statements is true? Choose **one** answer.

(a) Output tax should be charged on the sale of the van because the plumber is going to use it solely for business purposes	
(b) Output tax should be charged on the sale of the van because input VAT was claimed on its purchase	
(c) Output tax should not be charged on the sale of the van as the plumber is not registered for VAT	

(2) If the accountant of this business is not sure of the correct VAT treatment for the sale of the van which of the following actions should he take?

Choose **one** answer.

(a)	Ask the plumber who is purchasing the van what he believes to be the correct treatment	
(b)	Ask the owner of the business who is not an accountant whether the business should charge VAT	
(c)	Look on the HMRC website for guidance on this matter	

(e) Supplies purchased by a business from a country outside the EU are known as which of the following?

(a)	Acquisitions	
(b)	Imports	
(c)	Exports	
(d)	Disposals	

Task 5

(a)   Amroth Ltd sells goods at standard rate VAT of 20%. The net value of the supply made to a customer is £745.24. Amroth Ltd gives this customer a trade discount of 2.5%.

What is the amount of VAT to be shown on the invoice that Amroth Ltd will issue to this customer, correct to **two** decimal places?

£ [   ]

(b)   A business supplies one of its customers with standard-rated goods with a VAT-inclusive price of £275.

How much output VAT should the business include in its VAT account for this supply?

£ [   ]

(c)   At the end of the quarter the total value of the debits on a business's VAT Control Account is £12,431.22 and the value of the credits is £10,424.10. There was no balance brought down on the account at the beginning of the quarter.

When the business completes its VAT Return which of the following will be true?

(a) The business will pay HMRC £2,007.12	
(b) The business will claim a refund from HMRC of £2,007.12	
(c) The business will pay HMRC £10,424.10	
(d) The business will claim a refund from HMRC of £12,431.22	

Task 6

This task is about preparing figures for a business's VAT Return for the quarter ended 30 June 20-0.

The standard rate of VAT is 20%.

The following accounts have been extracted from the ledgers:

Sales account

Date 20-0	Reference	Debit £	Date 20-0	Reference	Credit £
30/06	Balance c/d	274,040.00	01/04 – 30/06	Sales day-book – UK sales	149,246.00
			01/04 – 30/06	Sales day-book – exports	41,250.00
			01/04 – 30/06	Cash-book – UK sales	83,544.00
	Total	274,040.00		Total	274,040.00

Purchases account

Date 20-0	Reference	Debit £	Date 20-0	Reference	Credit £
01/04 -30/06	Purchases day-book – UK purchases	125,420.00	30/06	Balance c/d	136,910.00
01/04 -30/06	Purchases day-book – zero-rated imports	11,490.00			
	Total	136,910.00		Total	136,910.00

VAT account

Date 20-0	Reference	Debit £	Date 20-0	Reference	Credit £
01/04 -30/06	Purchases day-book – UK purchases	25,084.00	01/04 -30/06	Sales day-book – UK sales	29,849.20
			01/04 -30/06	Cash-book – UK sales	16,708.80

You are told that bad debt relief on a sales invoice for £691.60 excluding VAT is to be claimed in this quarter.

(a) Calculate the figure to be claimed as bad debt relief on the VAT Return.

£ [   ]

(b) Calculate the figure for Box 1 of the VAT Return – once any necessary corrections have been made.

£ [   ]

(c) Calculate the figure for Box 4 of the VAT Return – once any necessary corrections have been made.

£ [   ]

(d) The business owner is considering importing goods from a country outside of the EU and has contacted the Finance Manager to ask how this should be treated for VAT purposes. Unfortunately the Finance Manager is out of the office and has asked you to respond to the owner. You are not familiar with this aspect of VAT and feel it is beyond your current expertise.

How should you respond to the Finance Manager?

(a)	'I'm afraid I don't know the answer so I cannot respond to the owner without discussing this with you.'
(b)	'I'm not sure of all the details but will advise the owner that it's pretty much the same as how we treat imports from EU countries.'
(c)	'I don't want to look stupid in front of the owner so I will tell him what I think might be the answer.'

Task 7

This task is about completing an online VAT Return for a business for the quarter ended 31 October 20-0.

The following accounts have been extracted from its ledgers:

Sales account

Date 20-0	Reference	Debit £	Date 20-0	Reference	Credit £
31/10	Balance c/d	487,127.00	01/08 -31/10	Sales day-book – UK sales	447,674.20
			01/08 -31/10	Sales day-book – exports	39,452.80
	Total	487,127.00		Total	487,127.00

Purchases account

Date 20-0	Reference	Debit £	Date 20-0	Reference	Credit £
01/08 -31/10	Purchases day-book – UK purchases	270,671.00	31/10	Balance c/d	289,397.10
01/08 -31/10	Purchases day-book – EU acquisitions	18,726.10			
	Total	289,397.10		Total	289,397.10

VAT account

Date 20-0	Reference	Debit £	Date 20-0	Reference	Credit £
01/08 -31/10	Purchases day-book – UK purchases	54,134.20	01/08 -31/10	Sales day-book – UK sales	89,534.84

You are told that all acquisitions are of items that attract VAT at the standard rate.

(a)   Enter the relevant figures into the online VAT Return for the period ended 31 October 20-0. Do not leave any box blank.

Online VAT Return for period ended 31 October 20-0		£
VAT due in this period on sales and other outputs	**Box 1**	
VAT due in this period on acquisitions from other EC Member States	**Box 2**	
Total VAT due (the sum of boxes 1 and 2)	**Box 3**	Calculated value
VAT reclaimed in the period on purchases and other inputs, including acquisitions from the EC	**Box 4**	
Net VAT to be paid to HMRC or reclaimed by you. (Difference between boxes 3 and 4.) (If Box 4 is greater than Box 3, use a minus sign.)	**Box 5**	Calculated value
Total value of sales and all other outputs excluding any VAT. Include your box 8 figure. WHOLE POUNDS ONLY	**Box 6**	
Total value of purchases and all other inputs excluding any VAT. Include your box 9 figure. WHOLE POUNDS ONLY	**Box 7**	
Total value of all supplies of goods and related costs, excluding any VAT, to other EC Member States. WHOLE POUNDS ONLY	**Box 8**	
Total value of all acquisitions of goods and related costs, excluding any VAT from other EC Member States. WHOLE POUNDS ONLY	**Box 9**	

(b)   Calculate the values that will be shown online when you submit the VAT Return for the following boxes. If a repayment is due, use a minus sign in Box 5.

Total VAT due (the sum of boxes 1 and 2) (Box 3): £

Net VAT to be paid to HMRC or reclaimed by you (difference between boxes 3 and 4) (Box 5): £

Task 8

You are an Accounts Assistant at Mattsam Ltd where you report to the Financial Controller. Below is the VAT Return that you have completed for the quarter ended 30 April 20-0.

Online VAT Return for period ended 30 April 20-0		£
VAT due in this period on sales and other outputs	Box 1	127451.80
VAT due in this period on acquisitions from other EC Member States	Box 2	7452.20
Total VAT due (the sum of boxes 1 and 2)	Box 3	Calculated value
VAT reclaimed in the period on purchases and other inputs, including acquisitions from the EC	Box 4	88464.00
Net VAT to be paid to HMRC or reclaimed by you. (Difference between boxes 3 and 4.) (If Box 4 is greater than Box 3, use a minus sign.)	Box 5	Calculated value
Total value of sales and all other outputs excluding any VAT. Include your box 8 figure. WHOLE POUNDS ONLY	Box 6	678759
Total value of purchases and all other inputs excluding any VAT. Include your box 9 figure. WHOLE POUNDS ONLY	Box 7	442320
Total value of all supplies of goods and related costs, excluding any VAT, to other EC Member States. WHOLE POUNDS ONLY	Box 8	41500
Total value of all acquisitions of goods and related costs, excluding any VAT from other EC Member States. WHOLE POUNDS ONLY	Box 9	37261

Mattsam Ltd does not operate any of the special accounting schemes.

Today's date is 12 May 20-0.

(a)   Draft an email to the Financial Controller of Mattsam Ltd advising him of the amount of VAT that will be paid or received and the date that it is due.

To

From

Date   12 May 20-0

Subject   Completed VAT Return

Please be advised that I have just completed the VAT Return for the quarter

ended

The VAT Return must be filed by

The amount of VAT **payable/receivable** (delete as appropriate) will be

£

Kind regards

Accounts Assistant

(b)   The Maintenance Manager at the business that you work for has asked you to provide him with £1,800 in cash to pay the decorating company that has repainted the business's meeting rooms. He tells you 'There will not be an invoice for this'; that way he can avoid the VAT.

Answer each of these questions YES or NO.

(1)   Is this ethical behaviour on the part of the Maintenance Manager?

YES / NO

(2)   Should you provide the Maintenance Manager with the cash he asked for?

YES / NO

Practice
assessment 2

Task 1

(a) Last year Charlize had a taxable turnover of £98,000; this year her taxable turnover has reduced to £70,000. Decide whether the following statement is true or false.

'Charlize should deregister for VAT immediately.'

TRUE / FALSE

(b) Sarah's turnover for the last year was £105,000. In which of the following circumstances should Sarah immediately register for VAT? Choose **one** option.

(a) All £105,000 is exempt from VAT	
(b) £60,000 is taxable at reduced rate VAT and £45,000 is exempt from VAT	
(c) £60,000 is taxable at standard rate VAT and £45,000 is zero-rated for VAT	

(c) A business reached the VAT registration threshold four months ago but did not register for VAT. Since that date it has invoiced customers £37,500 for standard-rated taxable supplies.

(1) How much must the business pay to HMRC in respect of output tax for the period that it was not registered?

£

(2) In these circumstances the customers are required to reimburse the business for the VAT that they have paid to HMRC for these sales.

TRUE / FALSE

Task 2

(a)   A credit note for taxable supplies a business has made is being processed. What will be the effect on VAT for the business? Choose **one** answer.

(a) Output tax will increase	
(b) Output tax will decrease	
(c) Input tax will increase	
(d) Input tax will decrease	

(b)   Predent Ltd is a VAT registered business that is trading with Microness Ltd on a pro-forma invoice basis. Microness Ltd issues a pro-forma invoice to Predent Ltd on 21 August. Predent Ltd pays on 27 August. Microness Ltd then delivers the goods on 1 September and the VAT invoice is then issued on 4 September.

What is the tax point for this transaction? Choose **one** option.

(a) 21 August	
(b) 27 August	
(c) 1 September	
(d) 4 September	

(c)   Enderphil Ltd supplies goods that are a mixture of zero-rated supplies and exempt supplies. Which of the following statements is true? Choose **one** answer.

(a) All of the input VAT can be reclaimed	
(b) None of the input VAT can be reclaimed	
(c) Some of the input VAT can be reclaimed, in proportion to the different types of supply	

(d)   A business makes the following mixed supply to a single customer:
   •   standard-rated goods for £97 plus VAT
   •   zero-rated goods for £75
   •   exempt goods for £38

Decide whether this business can issue a simplified invoice to this customer.

YES / NO

Task 3

(a) Reducto Ltd has an annual taxable turnover of £124,000 and makes an additional £37,000 of exempt supplies. Decide whether the following statement is true or false.

'Reducto Ltd is eligible to register for the flat rate scheme.'

TRUE / FALSE

(b) A business that is registered under the cash accounting scheme can also register under which of the following schemes as well? Choose **one** option.

(a)	Annual accounting scheme	
(b)	Flat rate scheme	

(c) The main reason a business registers for the flat rate scheme is which of the following? Select **one** option.

(a)	The business supplies zero-rated goods but most of its inputs are at standard rate VAT	
(b)	The business wants to charge its customers a flat rate of VAT that is less than the standard rate	
(c)	The business only makes exempt supplies so this is the only way it can reclaim input VAT	
(d)	The business wants to simplify its VAT affairs by calculating VAT at a single percentage rate on all its taxable outputs	

Task 4

(a)   Merlin has recently set up in business and has already registered for VAT. He makes the following purchases in the first three months of trading. For each of the purchases decide whether the input VAT can be reclaimed on the next VAT Return.

Tick **all** items on which the VAT can be reclaimed.

Item	Net value £	VAT £	Gross £	VAT reclaimable?
Company delivery van	13,000	2,600	15,600	
Entertaining prospective customers	435	87	522	
Staff party to celebrate a large customer order	275	55	330	
Carpet for the staff lounge	120	24	144	
New car for Merlin's wife who does one day of secretarial work for the business	9,300	1,860	11,160	

(b)   Tamsin is completing her VAT Return for the quarter ended 31 October. She realises that she has entered a sales invoice for £200 plus standard rate VAT as a purchase invoice.

She must make the necessary adjustment for this in the current VAT Return. What effect will this have on the VAT Return for the quarter ending 31 October? Choose **one** option.

(a) The net VAT will increase by £40	
(b) The net VAT will decrease by £40	
(c) The net VAT will decrease by £80	
(d) The net VAT will increase by £80	

(c)   HMRC rules mean that if a business finds an error in a previous quarter's VAT Return it must complete a VAT 652 'Notification of Errors in VAT Returns' in which of the following circumstances? Choose **one** option.

(a) Where the error is more than £10,000 or 1% of the business's quarterly turnover	
(b) Where the error is more than £10,000 or 1% of the business's annual turnover	
(c) Where the error is more than £50,000 or 1% of the business's quarterly turnover	
(d) Where the error is more than £50,000 or 1% of the business's annual turnover	

(d) An accountant who is responsible for completing a business's VAT Return and who keeps herself up-to-date with changes in VAT regulations is complying with which of these ethical principles.

Choose **one** answer.

(a) Confidentiality	
(b) Integrity	
(c) Professional competence and due care	

(e) 'A business that receives a surcharge liability notice issued by HMRC must pay a surcharge to HMRC.'

Decide whether the above statement is correct.

TRUE / FALSE

Task 5

(a)   Edrich Ltd sells goods at standard rate VAT. The net value of the supply made to a customer is £247.14. Edrich Ltd gives this customer a trade discount of 1.75%.

What is the amount of VAT to be shown on the invoice that Edrich Ltd will issue to this customer, correct to **two** decimal places?

£ _____

(b)   A business supplies a standard-rated item at a price of £785 excluding VAT. The customer pays for the item within 10 days and so takes advantage of an 8% prompt payment discount offered by the business.

How much output tax should the business include in its VAT account for this supply?

£ _____

(c)   Chesnie is a VAT registered trader. He is currently filing some of his receipts for items that have been paid for in cash. One receipt is for office stationery; the total amount paid was £127.38. The current rate of VAT is 20%. What will be the VAT and the net amount to be recorded in Chesnie's accounts?

Tick **one** amount for VAT and **one** net amount.

	VAT	Net amount
£21.23		
£25.47		
£106.15		
£127.38		

(d)   Rebecca is a VAT registered trader. She is currently completing her quarterly VAT Return and has realised that she omitted a reduced rate purchase of £1,278.90 including VAT. How much additional input VAT should be reclaimed from HMRC on her next VAT Return?

Which **one** of these options is correct?

(a) £255.78	
(b) £213.15	
(c) £63.94	
(d) £60.90	

Task 6

This task is about preparing figures for a business's VAT Return for the quarter ended 30 September 20-0.

The standard rate of VAT is 20%.

The following accounts have been extracted from the ledgers:

Sales account

Date 20-0	Reference	Debit £	Date 20-0	Reference	Credit £
30/09	Balance c/d	142,250.00	01/07 -30/09	Sales day-book – UK sales	111,900.00
			01/07 -30/09	Sales day-book – EU despatches	8,900.00
			01/07 -30/09	Cash-book – UK sales	21,450.00

VAT account

Date 20-0	Reference	Debit £	Date 20-0	Reference	Credit £
01/07 -30/09	Purchases day-book – UK purchases	13,496.00	01/07 -30/09	Sales day-book – UK sales	22,380.00
			01/07 -30/09	Cash-book – UK sales	4,290.00
			01/07 -30/09	Purchases returns day-book – UK purchases returns	1,270.00

You discover that during the VAT period the business has sold a delivery van for £4,140 including VAT of £690. The gross sales amount has been recorded in the sales account and no entry has been made in the VAT account.

(a)   The owner of the business has suggested that this is not significant and that you should ignore it when completing the VAT Return.

Which of the following should be your response to the owner of the business?

(a)	You're right this is not significant so I agree we should ignore it	
(b)	My ethical principles mean that I cannot ignore this matter	

(b)   Calculate the figure to be included in Box 1 of the VAT Return, once any necessary corrections to the ledger accounts have been made.

£ [   ]

(c)   Calculate the figure to be included in Box 4 of the VAT Return, once any necessary corrections to the ledger accounts have been made.

£ [   ]

(d)   Calculate the figure to be included in Box 6 of the VAT Return, once any necessary corrections to the ledger accounts have been made. Your figure should be in whole pounds only.

£ [   ]

Task 7

This task is about completing a VAT Return for a business for the quarter ended 30 June 20-0.

The following accounts have been extracted from its ledgers:

Sales account

Date 20-0	Reference	Debit £	Date 20-0	Reference	Credit £
30/06	Balance c/d	212,059.20	01/04 -30/06	Sales day-book – UK sales	198,608.20
			01/04 -30/06	Cash book – UK sales	13,451.00
	Total	212,059.20		Total	212,059.20

Purchases account

Date 20-0	Reference	Debit £	Date 20-0	Reference	Credit £
01/04 -30/06	Purchases day-book – UK purchases	212,541.00	30/06	Balance c/d	242,401.10
01/04 -30/06	Purchases day-book – EU acquisitions	29,860.10			
	Total	242,401.10		Total	242,401.10

VAT account

Date 20-0	Reference	Debit £	Date 20-0	Reference	Credit £
01/04 -30/06	Purchases day-book – UK purchases	42,508.20	01/04 -30/06	Sales day-book – UK sales	39,721.64
			01/04 -30/06	Cash book – UK sales	2,690.20

You are told that standard-rated purchases of £6,125 plus VAT were left off the previous VAT Return and must be included in this Return.

You are also told that all acquisitions are for items that attract VAT at standard rate.

(a) Enter the relevant figures into the online VAT Return for the period ended 30 June 20-0. Do not leave any box blank.

Online VAT Return for period ended 30 June 20-0		£
VAT due in this period on sales and other outputs	**Box 1**	
VAT due in this period on acquisitions from other EC Member States	**Box 2**	
Total VAT due (the sum of boxes 1 and 2)	**Box 3**	Calculated value
VAT reclaimed in the period on purchases and other inputs, including acquisitions from the EC	**Box 4**	
Net VAT to be paid to HMRC or reclaimed by you. (Difference between boxes 3 and 4.) (If Box 4 is greater than Box 3, use a minus sign.)	**Box 5**	Calculated value
Total value of sales and all other outputs excluding any VAT. Include your box 8 figure. WHOLE POUNDS ONLY	**Box 6**	
Total value of purchases and all other inputs excluding any VAT. Include your box 9 figure. WHOLE POUNDS ONLY	**Box 7**	
Total value of all supplies of goods and related costs, excluding any VAT, to other EC Member States. WHOLE POUNDS ONLY	**Box 8**	
Total value of all acquisitions of goods and related costs, excluding any VAT from other EC Member States. WHOLE POUNDS ONLY	**Box 9**	

(b) Calculate the values that will be shown online when you submit the VAT Return for the following boxes. If a repayment is due, use a minus sign in Box 5.

Total VAT due (the sum of boxes 1 and 2) (Box 3): £

Net VAT to be paid to HMRC or reclaimed by you (difference between boxes 3 and 4) (Box 5):   £

Task 8

You are an Assistant Accountant at Willmark Ltd where you report to the Financial Controller. Below is the VAT Return that you have completed for the quarter ended 31 May 20-0. Willmark Ltd does not operate any of the special accounting schemes and has a direct debit arrangement in place with HMRC for VAT payments.

Online VAT Return for quarter ended 31 May 20-0		£
VAT due in this period on sales and other outputs	Box 1	278561.23
VAT due in this period on acquisitions from other EC Member States	Box 2	3294.89
Total VAT due (the sum of boxes 1 and 2)	Box 3	Calculated value
VAT reclaimed in the period on purchases and other inputs, including acquisitions from the EC	Box 4	14743.02
Net VAT to be paid to HMRC or reclaimed by you. (Difference between boxes 3 and 4.) (If Box 4 is greater than Box 3, use a minus sign.)	Box 5	Calculated value
Total value of sales and all other outputs excluding any VAT. Include your box 8 figure. WHOLE POUNDS ONLY	Box 6	1392806
Total value of purchases and all other inputs excluding any VAT. Include your box 9 figure. WHOLE POUNDS ONLY	Box 7	1057240
Total value of all supplies of goods and related costs, excluding any VAT, to other EC Member States. WHOLE POUNDS ONLY	Box 8	0
Total value of all acquisitions of goods and related costs, excluding any VAT from other EC Member States. WHOLE POUNDS ONLY	Box 9	16474

Today's date is 8 June 20-0. Bank working days are Monday to Friday. There are no bank holidays in June or July.

(a) Draft an email to the Financial Controller of Willmark Ltd advising him of the amount of VAT that will be paid or received and the date that it is due.

To: [   ]

From: [   ]

Date: 8 June 20-0

Subject: **Completed VAT Return**

Please be advised that I have just completed the VAT Return for the quarter

ended [   ]

The VAT Return must be filed by [   ]

The amount of VAT **payable/to be received** (select one option) will be £ [   ]

Please arrange **to reclaim this amount in due course / to pay this electronically to arrive no later than 30 June / to pay this electronically to arrive no later than 7 July / for sufficient funds to be available for HMRC to direct debit the business account on 12 July.** (select one option)

Kind regards

Assistant accountant

(b)   The Sales Director is putting together a proposal for the owners of the business that includes some complex VAT calculations. The Finance Manager is on holiday so the Sales Director has asked you to provide her with some detailed VAT information to support the proposal. You are concerned about this and are not familiar with this aspect of VAT so feel it is beyond your current expertise.

How should you respond to the Sales Director?

(a)	'OK, no problem I'll give it a go.'	
(b)	'I don't know the answers but I'll have a quick look in my AAT books and I should be able to come up with the right information.'	
(c)	'I don't know the answer so I cannot advise you without guidance from the Finance Manager.'	

Practice
assessment 3

Task 1

(a) A business that is not currently registered for VAT makes only standard-rated supplies. Its sales over the last 12 months have been at a steady average of £6,000 a month. On 1 August the business accepts an order for £81,000 of goods to be delivered and invoiced at the end of August. The customer will be expected to pay for the goods within 30 days of receipt of the invoice.

Which **one** of the following statements most accurately describes the requirement on the business to register for VAT as at 1 August?

(a)	The business is not yet required to register as its taxable turnover for the past 12 months is below the VAT registration threshold
(b)	The business must register without delay because the new order plus the average month's sales is for an amount in excess of the VAT registration threshold
(c)	The business will exceed the VAT registration threshold in the 12 month period to 31 August and must register on 31 August

A VAT registered trader is unclear whether he can apply to operate the annual accounting scheme.

(b) Complete the following statement by selecting **one** option.

To find out more information about the annual accounting scheme for VAT, the trader should first of all …

(a)	… call HMRC on the General Enquiries helpline
(b)	… write to HMRC
(c)	… look at the HMRC website

(c) Complete the following statement by selecting **one** option.

Voluntary registration for VAT is available for any business …

(a)	… that has been trading for more than three years
(b)	… that makes at least some taxable supplies
(c)	… with taxable turnover greater than the VAT registration threshold

Task 2

A VAT registered business sells a variety of standard-rated and zero-rated items and wishes to issue simplified invoices.

(a) Which **one** of the following statements is TRUE?

(a)	The business may issue a simplified invoice for standard-rated items of £215 plus VAT
(b)	The business may issue a simplified invoice for a mixed supply of zero-rated items of £80 and standard-rated items of £150 plus VAT
(c)	The business may issue a simplified invoice for a mixed supply of standard-rated items of £140 including VAT and zero-rated items of £100

(b) Which **one** of the following items of information can be omitted from a simplified invoice?

(a)	The amount of VAT
(b)	The tax point
(c)	The seller's VAT registration number
(d)	The seller's address
(e)	A description of the goods and services

(c) A VAT registered business makes both standard-rated supplies and exempt supplies. The amount of input tax incurred relating to its exempt supplies is above the minimum 'de minimis' amount.

Which **one** of the following statements is TRUE?

(a)	All its input tax can be reclaimed because the 'de minimis' amount is exceeded
(b)	None of its input tax can be reclaimed because the 'de minimis' amount is exceeded
(c)	A proportion of the input tax can be reclaimed, in relation to the different types of supply

(d) A business delivers goods to a customer on 15 May and issues a VAT invoice on 21 May.

What is the tax point for this supply? Select **one** option.

(a)	15 May
(b)	21 May

(e)   A business has a 12 month contract to provide security services to its client on a continuous basis. It invoices the business at the end of each month.

Decide which of the following statements is correct. Choose **one** option.

(a) The tax point for this service is created at the end of the 12 month contract	
(b) A tax point is created every time the business issues an invoice to its client	

Task 3

A VAT registered business operates a single special accounting scheme for VAT and has the following characteristics:

- the business has a taxable turnover of £750,000 per year.
- the business only pays output tax to HMRC when it has been received from its customers.
- the business only reclaims input tax from HMRC when it has been paid to its suppliers.
- the business cannot claim bad debt relief.

(a)   Which **one** of the following schemes is being used?

(a) The cash accounting scheme	
(b) The annual accounting scheme	
(c) The flat rate scheme	

(b)   A VAT registered trader is using the annual accounting scheme.

Which other special accounting scheme can be operated with the annual accounting scheme?

(a) The cash accounting scheme	
(b) The flat rate scheme	
(c) None	
(d) The cash accounting scheme or the flat rate scheme but not both	

(c)   Decide whether the following statement is true or false. 'Bad debt relief is only available when a debt has been written off by a business and is at least twelve months old.'

TRUE / FALSE

(d)   A bookkeeper that uses the flat rate scheme for VAT but that is classified as a limited cost business must use which of the following flat rates?

(a) 5%	
(b) 14.5%	
(c) 16.5%	
(d) 20%	

Task 4

(a) A business has just discovered that it has made the following non-deliberate, non-careless errors that affect its previous VAT Return:

- VAT of £121 on a purchase invoice from a UK supplier was entered twice in the accounting records.

- VAT of £74 on a credit note received from a UK supplier was not recorded in the accounts of the business.

The business is permitted to correct the net error on the current VAT Return.

Which of the following corrections should the business make to Box 4 of its current VAT Return? Choose **one** answer.

(a) Add £195	
(b) Add £47	
(c) Deduct £195	
(d) Deduct £47	

(b) A business has received a surcharge liability notice from HMRC.

(1) Which of the following statements is correct?

(a)	The notice would only have been issued if the business had missed the deadline for submitting its VAT Return and paying any VAT due	
(b)	The notice would only have been issued if the business had failed to register for VAT at the correct time	
(c)	The notice would only have been issued if the business had decided to deregister for VAT	

(2) Complete the following sentence by inserting the correct number.

'A surcharge liability notice from HMRC puts the business in a surcharge period for

[   ] months.'

(c) A business owner has recently purchased a van for his family to use for surfing holidays. He has asked the accountant to process the invoice for the van through the business's accounts and reclaim the VAT in the usual way.

Which of the following is the ethical approach to take in this situation?

(a) Immediately report the owner of the business to HMRC	
(b) Explain to the owner that as this is personal expenditure it is disallowed for VAT so the VAT cannot be reclaimed	

(d) **(1)** Supplies made by a UK business to a business from a country outside the EU are known as which of the following?

(a)	Acquisitions	
(b)	Imports	
(c)	Exports	
(d)	Disposals	

(2) Complete the following sentence by circling the correct word in bold.

'A supply is normally zero-rated if it is to a business that is not VAT registered but is **within / outside** the EU.'

Task 5

(a) A VAT registered business that sells health products supplies a trade customer with the following items:

- Zero-rated items for £375

- Standard-rated items for £893 plus VAT

A trade discount of 3% is offered.

How much VAT should be included on the invoice? Choose **one** option.

(a) £245.99	
(b) £178.60	
(c) £173.24	
(d) £75.00	

(b) A business supplies a standard-rated item at a price of £788 excluding VAT. The customer is entitled to a 5% trade discount and pays for the item within 10 days which allows it to take advantage of an 8% prompt payment discount offered by the business.

How much output tax should the business include in its VAT account for this supply?

£ _____

(c) A VAT registered business is processing the two credit notes issued to customers that are detailed below.

Credit note 1: Total value £127.26 including standard VAT

Credit note 2: Total value £94.29 including reduced rate VAT

By how much will these two credit notes reduce the output VAT for the business?

Which **one** of these options is correct?

(a) £36.92	
(b) £30.16	
(c) £25.70	
(d) £21.21	

Task 6

This task is about preparing figures for a business's VAT Return for the period ended 30 April.

The standard rate of VAT is 20%.

The following accounts have been extracted from the business's ledgers:

Purchases account

Date 20-0	Reference	Debit £	Date 20-0	Reference	Credit £
01/02 -30/04	Purchases day-book – UK purchases	328,091.50	30/04	Balance c/d	356,181.86
01/02 -30/04	Purchases day-book – zero rated imports	28,090.36			
	Total	356,181.86		Total	356,181.86

VAT account

Date 20-0	Reference	Debit £	Date 20-0	Reference	Credit £
01/02 -30/04	Purchases day-book – UK purchases	65,618.30	01/02 -30/04	Sales day-book – UK sales	30,705.57
			01/02 -30/04	Cash-book – UK sales	2,057.17

You are told that UK purchases included a delivery van for £27,750 plus VAT and a company car for the Sales Director which he will use for business and private use for £36,250 plus VAT. The related VAT for both purchases is included in the VAT account figure.

(a) Calculate the figure for Box 1 of the VAT Return – once any necessary corrections have been made.

£ [   ]

(b) Calculate the figure for Box 4 of the VAT Return – once any necessary corrections have been made.

£ [   ]

(c) Calculate the figure for Box 7 of the VAT Return – once any necessary corrections have been made.

£ [   ]

Task 7

This task is about preparing all the figures for completion of a business's online VAT Return for the period ended 30 June 20-0.

The following accounts have been extracted from the business's ledgers:

Sales account

Date 20-0	Reference	Debit £	Date 20-0	Reference	Credit £
30/06	Balance c/d	389,184.50	01/04 -30/06	Sales day-book – UK sales	372,990.60
			01/04 -30/06	Sales day-book – EU despatches	16,193.90
	Total	389,184.50		Total	389,184.50

Purchases account

Date 20-0	Reference	Debit £	Date 20-0	Reference	Credit £
01/04 -30/06	Purchases day-book – UK purchases	136,799.05	01/04 -30/06	Balance c/d	143,637.69
01/04 -30/06	Purchases day-book – zero-rated imports	6,838.64			
	Total	143,637.69		Total	143,637.69

VAT account

Date 20-0	Reference	Debit £	Date 20-0	Reference	Credit £
01/04 -30/06	Purchases day-book – UK purchases	27,359.81	01/04 -30/06	Sales day-book – UK sales	74,598.12

You are told that standard-rated sales of £5,473.80 plus VAT were left off the previous VAT Return and have to be included in this Return.

(a) Enter the relevant figures into the online VAT Return for the period ended 30 June 20-0. Do not leave any box blank.

Online VAT Return for period ended 30 June 20-0		£
VAT due in this period on sales and other outputs	**Box 1**	
VAT due in this period on acquisitions from other EC Member States	**Box 2**	
Total VAT due (the sum of boxes 1 and 2)	**Box 3**	Calculated value
VAT reclaimed in the period on purchases and other inputs, including acquisitions from the EC	**Box 4**	
Net VAT to be paid to HMRC or reclaimed by you. (Difference between boxes 3 and 4). (If Box 4 is greater than Box 3, use a minus sign.)	**Box 5**	Calculated value
Total value of sales and all other outputs excluding any VAT. Include your box 8 figure. WHOLE POUNDS ONLY	**Box 6**	
Total value of purchases and all other inputs excluding any VAT. Include your box 9 figure. WHOLE POUNDS ONLY	**Box 7**	
Total value of all supplies of goods and related costs, excluding any VAT, to other EC Member States. WHOLE POUNDS ONLY	**Box 8**	
Total value of all acquisitions of goods and related costs, excluding any VAT from other EC Member States. WHOLE POUNDS ONLY	**Box 9**	

(b) Calculate the values that will be shown online when you submit the VAT Return for the following boxes. If a repayment is due, use a minus sign in Box 5.

Total VAT due (the sum of boxes 1 and 2) (Box 3): £

Net VAT to be paid to HMRC or reclaimed by you (difference between boxes 3 and 4) (Box 5): £

Task 8

(a)   You are an Accounting Technician who works for a restaurant and you report to the Financial Controller. You have been asked to advise him on how a decrease in the rate of VAT would affect the restaurant and what action would have to be taken as a consequence.

Today's date is 8 December.

Prepare a draft email to the Financial Controller providing information about some of the potential effects and consequences of a change. Choose **one** option to complete each sentence.

To:	**(Accounting technician/Financial controller)**
From:	**(Accounting technician/Financial controller)**
Date:	8 December

As the VAT rate is decreasing the business must consider whether the menu prices it charges to customers, which are, of course inclusive of VAT, should change. These prices **cannot change until the date of the next VAT Return / must change on the date of the VAT change / can remain unchanged if the business chooses**.

The new rate of VAT must be reflected in the amount of VAT we pay to HMRC **only if we change the prices to customers / whether we change the prices to customers or not / only if customers choose to pay the new prices.**

If the date of the change in VAT rate falls during one of our VAT periods, our system must **apply a single rate of VAT during that VAT period / apply both the old and the new rates of VAT during that VAT period depending on the size of the customer's bill / apply both the old and the new rates of VAT during that VAT period depending on the date of each meal.**

Kind regards

A Technician

(b)   You have recently completed the VAT Return for the business that you work for and discovered a large error that may result in a misdeclaration penalty if you report it to anyone. You are very concerned about your job if you admit this error. What is the ethical course of action that you should take in this situation?

Choose **one** answer.

(a)	Do not tell anyone and hope that the error is not discovered	
(b)	Correct the error on the current VAT Return despite knowing that it should be separately disclosed	
(c)	Explain to the Finance Manager that you have made the error and that the business must make a voluntary disclosure	

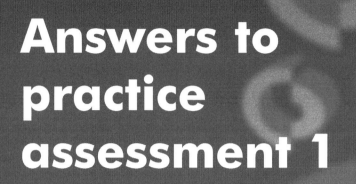

Answers to practice assessment 1

Task 1

(a)   (a)   The business will not have to register for VAT in the next year but can do so voluntarily

(b)

	Ranking
Telephone the HMRC helpline	2
Write to HMRC	3
Search on the HMRC website	1

(c)   (a)   ... almost immediately

Task 2

(a)   FALSE

(b)   (b)   Both input tax and output tax will decrease

(c)   (a)   The tax point for the deposit is 25 January and for the balance is 28 January

(d)   17 September

(e)   (c)   If the exempt supplies are below the 'de minimis' limit all of the input tax can be reclaimed

Task 3

(a)   (c)   Annual accounting scheme

(b)   (a)   If this is the first time the business has made a late submission the business will only be required to pay a surcharge if it further defaults in the following 12 months

(c)   **(1)**   £390

      (2)   (d)   In its VAT period ending 30 November

Task 4

(a)   £7,007.93

(b)   (b)   HMRC will view this as a deliberate error and issue a penalty

(c)   FALSE

(d)   **(1)**   (b)   Output tax should be charged on the sale of the van because input VAT was claimed on its purchase

      (2)   (c)   Look on the HMRC website for guidance on this matter

(e)   (b)   Imports

Task 5

(a)   £145.32

(b)   £45.83

(c)   (b)   The business will claim a refund from HMRC of £2,007.12

Task 6

(a) £138.32

(b) £46,558

(c) £25,222.32

(d) (a) 'I'm afraid I don't know the answer so I cannot respond to the owner without discussing this with you.'

Task 7

(a)

Online VAT Return for period ended 31 October 20-0		£
VAT due in this period on sales and other outputs	**Box 1**	89534.84
VAT due in this period on acquisitions from other EC Member States	**Box 2**	3745.22
Total VAT due (the sum of boxes 1 and 2)	**Box 3**	Calculated value
VAT reclaimed in the period on purchases and other inputs, including acquisitions from the EC	**Box 4**	57879.42
Net VAT to be paid to HMRC or reclaimed by you. (Difference between boxes 3 and 4.) (If Box 4 is greater than Box 3, use a minus sign.)	**Box 5**	Calculated value
Total value of sales and all other outputs excluding any VAT. Include your box 8 figure. WHOLE POUNDS ONLY	**Box 6**	487127
Total value of purchases and all other inputs excluding any VAT. Include your box 9 figure. WHOLE POUNDS ONLY	**Box 7**	289397
Total value of all supplies of goods and related costs, excluding any VAT, to other EC Member States. WHOLE POUNDS ONLY	**Box 8**	0
Total value of all acquisitions of goods and related costs, excluding any VAT from other EC Member States. WHOLE POUNDS ONLY	**Box 9**	18726

(b) Box 3: £93280.06

Box 5: £35400.64

Task 8

(a)

To:	**Financial Controller**
From:	**Accounts Assistant**
Date:	12 May 20-0
Subject:	Completed VAT Return

Please be advised that I have just completed the VAT Return for the quarter ended **30 April 20-0**

The VAT Return must be filed by **7 June 20-0**

The amount of VAT **payable** will be **£46,440**

(b) **(1)** NO

(2) NO

Answers to practice assessment 2

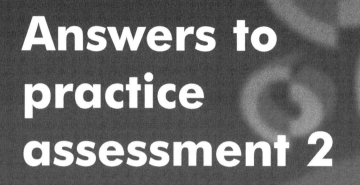

Task 1

(a) FALSE

(b) (c) £60,000 is taxable at standard rate VAT and £45,000 is zero-rated for VAT

(c) **(1)** £6,250

(2) FALSE

Task 2

(a) (b) Output tax will decrease

(b) (b) 27 August

(c) (c) Some of the input VAT can be reclaimed, in proportion to the different types of supply

(d) NO

Task 3

(a) TRUE

(b) (a) Annual accounting scheme

(c) (d) The business wants to simplify its VAT affairs by calculating VAT at a single percentage rate on all its taxable outputs

Task 4

(a)

Item	Net value £	VAT £	Gross £	VAT reclaimable?
Company delivery van	13,000	2,600	15,600	✔
Entertaining prospective customers	435	87	522	
Staff party to celebrate a large customer order	275	55	330	✔
Carpet for the staff lounge	120	24	144	✔
New car for Merlin's wife who does one day of secretarial work for the business	9,300	1,860	11,160	

(b) (d) The net VAT will increase by £80

(c) (a) Where the error is more than £10,000 or 1% of the business's quarterly turnover

(d) (c) Professional competence and due care

(e) FALSE

Task 5

(a)   £48.56

(b)   £144.44

(c)   VAT = £21.23 and net amount = £106.15

(d)   (d)   £60.90

Task 6

(a)   (b)   My ethical principles mean that I cannot ignore this matter

(b)   £27,360

(c)   £12,226

(d)   £141,560

Task 7

(a)

Online VAT Return for period ended 30 June 20-0		£
VAT due in this period on sales and other outputs	Box 1	42411.84
VAT due in this period on acquisitions from other EC Member States	Box 2	5972.02
Total VAT due (the sum of boxes 1 and 2)	Box 3	Calculated value
VAT reclaimed in the period on purchases and other inputs, including acquisitions from the EC	Box 4	49705.22
Net VAT to be paid to HMRC or reclaimed by you. (Difference between boxes 3 and 4.) (If Box 4 is greater than Box 3, use a minus sign.)	Box 5	Calculated value
Total value of sales and all other outputs excluding any VAT. Include your box 8 figure. WHOLE POUNDS ONLY	Box 6	212059
Total value of purchases and all other inputs excluding any VAT. Include your box 9 figure. WHOLE POUNDS ONLY	Box 7	248526
Total value of all supplies of goods and related costs, excluding any VAT, to other EC Member States. WHOLE POUNDS ONLY	Box 8	0
Total value of all acquisitions of goods and related costs, excluding any VAT from other EC Member States. WHOLE POUNDS ONLY	Box 9	29860

(b)   Box 3: £48383.86

   Box 5: –£1321.36

Task 8

To: **Financial Controller**

From: **Assistant Accountant**

Date: 8 June 20-0

Subject: **Completed VAT Return**

Please be advised that I have just completed the VAT Return for the quarter

ended **31 May 20-0**

The VAT Return must be filed by **7 July 20-0**

The amount of VAT **payable** will be £**267,113.10**

Please arrange **for sufficient funds to be available for HMRC to direct debit the business account on 12 July**.

Kind regards

Assistant accountant

(b)   (c) 'I don't know the answer so I cannot advise you without guidance from the Finance Manager.'

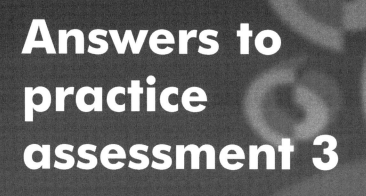

Answers to practice assessment 3

Task 1

(a)   (b)   The business must register without delay because the new order plus the average month's sales is for an amount in excess of the VAT registration threshold

(b)   (c)   To find out more information about the annual accounting scheme for VAT, the trader should first of all **look at the HMRC website**

(c)   (b)   Voluntary registration for VAT is available for any business **that makes at least some taxable supplies**

Task 2

(a)   (c)   The business may issue a simplified invoice for a mixed supply of standard-rated items of £140 including VAT and zero-rated items of £100

(b)   (a)   The amount of VAT

(c)   (c)   A proportion of the input tax can be reclaimed, in relation to the different types of supply

(d)   (b)   21 May

(e)   (b)   A tax point is created every time the business issues an invoice to its client

Task 3

(a)   (a)   The cash accounting scheme

(b)   (d)   The cash accounting scheme or the flat rate scheme but not both

(c)   FALSE

(d)   (c)   16.5%

Task 4

(a)   (c)   Deduct £195

(b)   **(1)**   (a)   The notice would only have been issued if the business had missed the deadline for submitting its VAT Return and paying any VAT due

          (2)   'A surcharge liability notice from HMRC puts the business in a surcharge period for **12** months.'

(c)   (b)   Explain to the owner that as this is personal expenditure it is disallowed for VAT so the VAT cannot be reclaimed

(d)   **(1)**   (c)   Exports

          (2)   'A supply is normally zero-rated if it is to a business that is not VAT registered but is **outside** the EU.'

Task 5

(a)   (c)   £173.24

(b)   £137.74

(c)   (c)   £25.70

Task 6

(a)   £32,762.74

(b)   £58,368.30

(c)   £356,181

Task 7

(a)

Online VAT Return for period ended 30 June 20-0		£
VAT due in this period on sales and other outputs	**Box 1**	75692.88
VAT due in this period on acquisitions from other EC Member States	**Box 2**	0.00
Total VAT due (the sum of boxes 1 and 2)	**Box 3**	Calculated value
VAT reclaimed in the period on purchases and other inputs, including acquisitions from the EC	**Box 4**	27359.81
Net VAT to be paid to HMRC or reclaimed by you. (Difference between boxes 3 and 4.) (If Box 4 is greater than Box 3, use a minus sign.)	**Box 5**	Calculated value
Total value of sales and all other outputs excluding any VAT. Include your box 8 figure. WHOLE POUNDS ONLY	**Box 6**	394658
Total value of purchases and all other inputs excluding any VAT. Include your box 9 figure. WHOLE POUNDS ONLY	**Box 7**	143637
Total value of all supplies of goods and related costs, excluding any VAT, to other EC Member States. WHOLE POUNDS ONLY	**Box 8**	16193
Total value of all acquisitions of goods and related costs, excluding any VAT from other EC Member States. WHOLE POUNDS ONLY	**Box 9**	0

(b)   Box 3: £75692.88

Box 5: £48333.07

Task 8

To: **Financial controller**
From: **Accounting technician**
Date: 8 December
As the VAT rate is decreasing the business must consider whether the menu prices it charges to customers, which are, of course inclusive of VAT, should change. These prices **can remain unchanged if the business chooses.**
The new rate of VAT must be reflected in the amount of VAT we pay to HMRC **whether we change the prices to customers or not.**
If the date of the change in VAT rate falls during one of our VAT periods, our system must **apply both the old and the new rates of VAT during that VAT period depending on the date of each meal.**
Kind regards,
A Technician

(b)   (c)   Explain to the Finance Manager that you have made the error and that the business must make a voluntary disclosure

Reference Material

for AAT Assessment of Indirect Tax

Finance Act 2018

For assessments from 1 January – 31 December 2019

Note: this reference material is accessible by candidates during their live computer-based assessment for Indirect Tax.

This material was current at the time this book was published, but may be subject to change. Readers are advised to check the AAT website or Osborne Books website for any updates.

Reference material for AAT assessment of Indirect Tax

Introduction

This document comprises data that you may need to consult during your Indirect Tax computer-based assessment.

The material can be consulted during the sample and live assessments through pop-up windows. It is made available here so you can familiarise yourself with the content before the test.

Do not take a print of this document into the exam room with you*.

This document may be changed to reflect periodical updates in the computer-based assessment, so please check you have the most recent version while studying. This version is based on Finance Act 2018 and is for use in AAT assessments 1 January – 31 December 2019.

*Unless you need a printed version as part of reasonable adjustments for particular needs, in which case you must discuss this with your tutor at least six weeks before the assessment date.

Contents

Introduction to VAT

VAT is a tax that's charged on most goods and services that VAT-registered businesses provide in the UK. It's also charged on goods and some services that are imported from countries outside the European Union (EU), and brought into the UK from other EU countries.

VAT is charged when a VAT-registered business sells taxable goods and services to either another business or to a non-business customer. This is called output tax.

When a VAT-registered business buys taxable goods or services for business use it can generally reclaim the VAT it has paid. This is called input tax.

Her Majesty's Revenue and Customs (HMRC) is the government department responsible for operating the VAT system. Payments of VAT collected are made by VAT-registered businesses to HMRC.

Rates of VAT

There are three rates of VAT, depending on the goods or services the business provides. The rates are:
  * standard – 20%. The standard-rate VAT fraction for calculating the VAT element of a gross supply is 20/120 or 1/6
  * reduced – 5%.
  * zero – 0%

There are also some goods and services that are:
  * exempt from VAT
  * outside the scope of VAT (outside the UK VAT system altogether)

Taxable supplies

Zero-rated goods and services count as taxable supplies and are part of taxable turnover, but no VAT is added to the selling price because the VAT rate is 0%.

If the business sells goods and services that are exempt, no VAT is added as they're not taxable supplies and they're also not taxable turnover.

Generally, a business can't register for VAT or reclaim the VAT on purchases if it only sells exempt goods and services. Where some of its supplies are of exempt goods and services, the business is referred to as partially exempt. It may not be able to reclaim the VAT on all of its purchases.

A business which buys and sells only - or mainly - zero-rated goods or services can apply to HMRC to be exempt from registering for VAT. This could make sense if the business pays little or no VAT on purchases.

Taxable turnover

Taxable turnover consists of standard-rated sales plus all reduced-rated and zero-rated sales but excludes the VAT on those sales, exempt sales and out-of-scope sales. If one VAT-registered business acquires another business it immediately absorbs the turnover of that business, whether the acquired business is registered for VAT or not. All VAT decisions must thereafter be made based on the combined turnover.

Change in VAT rate

Generally a business must use the VAT rate applicable from the time of the legislative change, unless payment has already been received or the goods have already been delivered. In these cases a tax point has already been created and the rate applicable will have been set by the tax point.

An exception arises where the goods have been delivered, or otherwise removed by the customer, the supplier has elected to follow the 14-day rule for issuing VAT invoices and the VAT rate increases between the date of delivery of the goods and the issuing of the invoice. In this case it is the new VAT rate which applies.

Immediately after the rate change a business may opt to honour supplies of goods and services at the rate which applied when the contract to supply was agreed, however output tax is still accountable at the new rate.

If the business offers a prompt payment discount and opts to issue a credit note to cover the reduction in payment made by the customer then a change in VAT rate which occurs between the

issue of the original invoice and final payment will not be affected by the change in VAT rate. The rate due on the credit note, issued to account for the reduced payment made, will be fixed by the tax point of the original invoice.

Registration and deregistration

Registration threshold

If, as at the end of any month, taxable turnover for the previous 12 months is more than the current registration threshold of £85,000, the business must register for VAT within 30 days. Registration without delay is required if, at any time, the value of taxable turnover in the next 30 day period alone is expected to be more than the registration threshold.

A business which has trading that temporarily takes it above the VAT threshold of £85,000 but which expects turnover to drop back below the threshold almost immediately can apply to stay unregistered, but the business must be able to prove to HMRC that the momentary increase is a true one-off occurrence.

If trading is below the registration threshold

If taxable turnover hasn't crossed the registration threshold, the business can still apply to register for VAT voluntarily.

Deregistration threshold

The deregistration threshold is £83,000. If taxable turnover for the previous 12 months is less than or equal to £83,000, or if it is expected to fall to £83,000 or less in the next 12 months, the business can either:
- voluntarily remain registered for VAT, or
- ask HMRC for its VAT registration to be cancelled

Failure to register

A business which fails to register when it is required to do so may face a civil penalty. More importantly HMRC will treat the business as though it had registered on time and will expect VAT to be accounted for as if it had been charged. The business has two choices in respect of this VAT, which it has not included in its invoices.

It may either:

- Allow HMRC to treat the invoices as VAT inclusive and absorb the VAT which should have been charged, OR
- Account for VAT as an addition to the charges already invoiced and attempt to recover this VAT from its customers.

Cancellation of VAT registration

A registration must be cancelled if the business is closed down or ceases to make taxable supplies.

If a business is being taken over by a business with a completely different structure, for example an unincorporated business being taken over by an incorporated business or vice versa, the original registration must be cancelled. It will either be replaced by a new registration for the new business, or be subsumed into the registration of the expanded business. In some circumstances the new business may apply for the registration of the business being taken over to be re-allocated to the new business. This may happen because two businesses merge and only one is currently registered. Re-allocation of the existing registration may be the most appropriate method of dealing with VAT registration.

Changes to the VAT registration

Some business changes will necessitate a change in details of the VAT registration, such as a change in the trading name or the address of the business. Other reasons for changes to the registration are a change in main business activities, particularly if this means a significant change to the types of supply, and changes to the business bank account details.

Failure to notify HMRC of changes which either cancel or change registration within 30 days of the relevant change may render the business and its owners liable to a civil penalty.

Keeping business records and VAT records

All VAT-registered businesses must keep certain business and VAT records.

These records are not required to be kept in a set way, provided they:
- are complete and up to date
- allow the correct amount of VAT owed to HMRC or by HMRC to be worked out
- are easily accessible when an HMRC visit takes place, eg the figures used to fill in the VAT Return must be easy to find

Business records

Business records which must be kept include the following:
- annual accounts, including statements of profit or loss
- bank statements and paying-in slips
- cash books and other account books
- orders and delivery notes
- purchases and sales day books
- records of daily takings such as till rolls
- relevant business correspondence

VAT records

In addition to these business records, VAT records must be kept.

In general, the business must keep the following VAT records:
- Records of all the standard-rated, reduced-rated, zero-rated and exempt goods and services that are bought and sold.
- Copies of all sales invoices issued. However, businesses do not have to keep copies of any less detailed (simplified) VAT invoices for items under £250 including VAT
- All purchase invoices for items purchased for business purposes unless the gross value of the supply is £25 or less and the purchase was from a coin-operated telephone or vending machine, or for car parking charges or tolls.
- All credit notes and debit notes received.
- Copies of all credit notes and debit notes issued.
- Records of any goods or services bought for which there is no VAT reclaim, such as business entertainment.
- Records of any goods exported.
- Any adjustments, such as corrections to the accounts or amended VAT invoices.

Generally all business records that are relevant for VAT must be kept for at least six years. If this causes serious problems in terms of storage or costs, then HMRC may allow some records to be kept for a shorter period. Records may be stored digitally especially if that is needed to overcome storage and access difficulties.

Keeping a VAT account

A VAT account is the separate record that must be kept of the VAT charged on taxable sales (referred to as output tax or VAT payable) and the VAT paid on purchases (called input tax or VAT reclaimable). It provides the link between the business records and the VAT Return. A VAT-registered business needs to add up the VAT in the sales and purchases records and then transfer these totals to the VAT account, using separate headings for VAT payable and VAT reclaimable.

The VAT account can be kept in whatever way suits the business best, as long as it includes information about the VAT that it:
- owes on sales, including when fuel scale charges are used
- owes on acquisitions from other European Union (EU) countries
- owes following a correction or error adjustment
- can reclaim on business purchases
- can reclaim on acquisitions from other EU countries
- can reclaim following a correction or error adjustment
- is reclaiming via VAT bad debt relief

The business must also keep records of any adjustments that have been made, such as balancing payments for the annual accounting scheme for VAT.

Information from the VAT account can be used to complete the VAT Return at the end of each accounting period. VAT reclaimable is subtracted from the VAT payable, to give the net amount of VAT to pay to or reclaim from HMRC.

Unless it is using the cash accounting scheme, a business:
- must pay the VAT charged on invoices to customers during the accounting period that relates to the return, even if those customers have not paid the invoices
- may reclaim the VAT charged on invoices from suppliers during the accounting period that relates to the return, even if it has not paid the invoices.

Exempt and partly-exempt businesses

Exempt goods and services

There are some goods and services on which VAT is not charged.

Exempt supplies are not taxable for VAT, so sales of exempt goods and services are not included in taxable turnover for VAT purposes. If a registered business buys exempt items, there is no VAT to reclaim.

(This is different to zero-rated supplies. In both cases VAT is not added to the selling price, but zero-rated goods or services are taxable for VAT at 0%, and are included in taxable turnover.)

Businesses which only sell or supply exempt goods or services

A business which only supplies goods or services that are exempt from VAT is called an exempt business. It cannot register for VAT, so it won't be able to reclaim any input tax on business purchases.

(Again this is different to zero-rated supplies, as a business can reclaim the input tax on any purchases that relate to zero-rated sales. In addition, a business which sells mainly or only zero-rated items may apply for an exemption from VAT registration, but then it can't claim back any input tax.)

Reclaiming VAT in a partly-exempt business

A business that is registered for VAT but that makes some exempt supplies is referred to as partly, or partially, exempt.

Generally, such businesses won't be able to reclaim the input tax paid on purchases that relate to exempt supplies.

However if the amount of input tax incurred relating to exempt supplies is below a minimum 'de minimus' amount, input tax can be reclaimed in full.

If the amount of input tax incurred relating to exempt supplies is above the 'de minimus' amount, only the part of the input tax that related to non-exempt supplies can be reclaimed.

Place of supply

Businesses which make supplies of goods and services to other member states of the EU or to countries outside the EU, or which receive goods and services from other member states of the EU or from countries outside the EU, must apply the "place of supply" rules for both goods and services. Place of supply is important because it drives the amount of VAT, if any, which is to be added to the cost of the services, and the manner in which any VAT is accounted for.

The place of supply is the place, or country, where the supply is made.

The following rules apply to a supplier based in the UK, with no alternative location elsewhere in the EU or outside the EU.

Supplies and receipts of goods

The place of supply for goods is always the country where the goods originate. This applies whether the goods are for the enjoyment of a business customer or a domestic customer.

Supplies and receipts of services

Supplies of services are covered by the "Place of supply of services order" or POSSO. Here the place of supply can be different depending on who the customer is, and whether the supply of services is within, or outside, the EU.

When the customer is a business customer the place of supply is where the customer is.

Should the customer be either:
- a non-business,
- an unregistered business, or
- a registered business, but the supply is of a non-business nature

then the place of supply is the country where the supplier is, irrespective of where the customer is.

Tax points

The time of supply, known as the 'tax point', is the date when a transaction takes place for VAT purposes. This date is not necessarily the date the supply physically takes place.

Generally, a registered business must pay or reclaim VAT in the (usually quarterly) VAT period, or tax period, in which the time of supply occurs, and it must use the correct rate of VAT in force on that date. This means knowing the time of supply/tax point for every transaction is important, as it must be put on the right VAT Return.

Time of supply (tax point) for goods and services

The time of supply for VAT purposes is defined as follows.
- For transactions where no VAT invoice is issued, the time of supply is normally the date the supply takes place (as defined below).
- For transactions where there is a VAT invoice, the time of supply is normally the date the invoice is issued, even if this is after the date the supply took place (as defined below).

To issue a VAT invoice, it must be sent (by post, email etc) or given to the customer for them to keep. A tax point cannot be created simply by preparing an invoice.

However there are exceptions to these rules on time of supply, detailed below.

Date the supply takes place

For goods, the time when the goods are considered to be supplied for VAT purposes is the date when one of the following happens.
- The supplier sends the goods to the customer.
- The customer collects the goods from the supplier.
- The goods (which are not either sent or collected) are made available for the customer to use, for example if the supplier is assembling something on the customer's premises.

For services, the date when the services are supplied for VAT purposes is the date when the service is carried out and all the work - except invoicing - is finished.

Exceptions regarding time of supply (tax point)

The above general principles for working out the time of supply do not apply in the following situations.

- For transactions where a VAT invoice is issued, or payment is received, in advance of the date of supply, the time of supply is the date the invoice is issued or the payment is received, whichever is the earlier.

- If the supplier receives full payment before the date when the supply takes place and no VAT invoice has yet been issued, the time of supply is the date the payment is received.

- If the supplier receives part-payment before the date when the supply takes place, the time of supply becomes the date the part-payment is received but only for the amount of the part-payment (assuming no VAT invoice has been issued before this date - in which case the time of supply is the date the invoice is issued). The time of supply for the remainder will follow the normal rules - and might fall in a different VAT period, and so have to go onto a different VAT Return.

- If the supplier issues a VAT invoice more than 14 days after the date when the supply took place, the time of supply will be the date the supply took place, and not the date the invoice is issued. However, if a supplier has genuine commercial difficulties in invoicing within 14 days of the supply taking place, they can contact HMRC to ask for permission to issue invoices later than 14 days and move the time of supply to this later date.

- Where services are being supplied on a continuous basis over a period in excess of a month but invoices are being issued regularly throughout the period. A tax point is created every time an invoice is issued or a payment is made, whichever happens first. A business may issue invoices for a whole 12 month period but only if it is known that payments will be made regularly.

- Goods supplied to a customer on a sale or return basis remain the property of the supplier until the customer indicates they are intending to keep them. If a time limit has been fixed for the sale or return the tax point is:

  ○ Where the fixed period is 12 months or less – the date the time limit expires
  ○ Where the fixed period is more than 12 months, or there is no fixed period – 12 months from the date the goods were sent
  ○ Where the customer adopts the goods before the fixed period has expired – the date the goods are adopted.

A payment made, which is not returnable, normally indicates that the goods have been adopted, however the receipt of a deposit which is repayable if the goods are returned is not an indication of adoption.

VAT invoices

To whom is a VAT invoice issued?

Whenever a VAT-registered business supplies taxable goods or services to another VAT-registered business, it must give the customer a VAT invoice.

A VAT-registered business is not required to issue a VAT invoice to a non-registered business or to a member of the public, but it must do so if requested.

What is a VAT invoice?

A VAT invoice shows certain VAT details of a supply of goods or services. It can be either in paper or electronic form. An electronic invoice (e-invoice) is only valid if it is in a secure format, for example a "pdf".

A VAT-registered customer must have a valid VAT invoice from the supplier in order to claim back the VAT they have paid on the purchase for their business.

What is NOT a VAT invoice?

The following are NOT VAT invoices:
- pro-forma invoices
- invoices for only zero-rated or exempt supplies
- invoices that state 'this is not a VAT invoice'
- statements of account
- delivery notes
- orders
- letters, emails or other correspondence

A registered business cannot reclaim the VAT it has paid on a purchase by using these documents as proof of payment.

What a VAT invoice must show

A VAT invoice must show:
- an invoice number which is unique and follows on from the number of the previous invoice - any spoiled or cancelled serially numbered invoice must be kept to show to a VAT officer at the next VAT inspection
- the seller's name or trading name, and address
- the seller's VAT registration number
- the invoice date
- the time of supply or tax point if this is different from the invoice date
- the customer's name or trading name, and address
- a description sufficient to identify the goods or services supplied to the customer

For each different type of item listed on the invoice, the business must show:
- the unit price or rate, excluding VAT
- the quantity of goods or the extent of the services
- the rate of VAT that applies to what is being sold
- the total amount payable, excluding VAT
- the rate of any cash or settlement discount
- the total amount of VAT charged

If the business issues a VAT invoice that includes zero-rated or exempt goods or services, it must:
- show clearly that there is no VAT payable on those goods or services
- show the total of those values separately

Where a prompt payment discount (PPD) is offered VAT must be accounted for to HMRC on the actual consideration received. The business must decide how to express this on the invoice. It may:
- invoice at the discounted value with VAT on that amount and then issue an additional invoice for the discount plus VAT at the point it becomes clear the customer will not take the discount by paying within the prompt payment period, OR
- invoice for the full value with VAT on that amount and then issue a credit note for the discount plus VAT should the customer pay the discounted value within the prompt payment period, OR
- invoice for the full value of the supply and associated VAT but provide information to the customer which allows it to determine how much to pay if they make payment within the prompt payment discount period. This information must include details of the input tax which they are permitted to recover depending on when they make payment. A warning should be included to the customer that failure to account for the correct amount of VAT is an offence.

Rounding on VAT invoices

The total VAT payable on all goods and services shown on a VAT invoice may be rounded down to a whole penny. Any fraction of a penny can be ignored. (This concession is not available to retailers.)

Time limits for issuing VAT invoices

There is a strict time limit on issuing VAT invoices. Normally a VAT invoice to a VAT-registered customer must be issued within 30 days of the basic tax point, which is either the date of supply of the goods or services, subject to the 14 day rule or, if the business was paid in advance, the date payment was received. This is so the customer can claim back the VAT on the supply, if they are entitled to do so.

The 30 day limit for goods starts with the day the goods are sent to the customer or taken by the customer or made available to the customer.

Invoices cannot be issued any later without permission from HMRC, except in a few limited circumstances.

A valid VAT invoice is needed to reclaim VAT

Even if a business is registered for VAT, it can normally only reclaim VAT on purchases if:
- they are for use in the business or for business purposes and
- a valid VAT invoice for the purchase is received and retained*.

*Subject to the rules for VAT invoices for supplies of £250 or less including VAT and for supplies of £25 including VAT or less:
- A simplified invoice for supplies of £250 or less is acceptable as a "valid VAT invoice" for input tax reclaim.
- Supplies of £25 or less including VAT, supported by a simple till receipt, can be assumed to be acceptable as a "valid VAT invoice" for input tax reclaim as long as the business has a reasonable understanding that the supplier is VAT registered.

Only VAT-registered businesses can issue valid VAT invoices. A business cannot reclaim VAT on any goods or services that are purchased from a business that is not VAT-registered.

Where simplified (less detailed) VAT invoices can be issued

Simplified VAT invoices

If a VAT-registered business makes taxable supplies of goods or services for £250 or less including VAT, then it can issue a simplified (less detailed) VAT invoice that only needs to show:
- the seller's name and address
- the seller's VAT registration number
- the time of supply (tax point)
- a description of the goods or services
- the total payable including VAT

If the supply includes items at different VAT rates then, for each different VAT rate, the simplified VAT invoice must also show the VAT rate applicable to the item(s).

Exempt supplies must not be included on a simplified VAT invoice.

There is no requirement for the business making the supply to keep copies of any less detailed invoices it has issued.

Pro-forma invoices

If there is a need to issue a sales document for goods or services not supplied yet, the business can issue a 'pro-forma' invoice or a similar document as part of the offer to supply goods or services to customers.

A pro-forma invoice is not a VAT invoice, and it should be clearly marked with the words "This is not a VAT invoice".

If a potential customer accepts the goods or services offered to them and these are actually supplied, then a VAT invoice must be issued within the appropriate time limit if appropriate.

If the business has been issued with a pro-forma invoice by a supplier it cannot be used to claim back VAT on the purchase. A VAT invoice must be obtained from the supplier.

Advance payments or deposits

An advance payment, or deposit, is a proportion of the total selling price that a customer pays before they are supplied with goods or services. When a business asks for an advance payment or deposit, the tax point is whichever of the following happens first:
- the date a VAT invoice is issued for the advance payment
- the date the advance payment is received

The business must include the VAT on the advance payment or deposit on the VAT Return for the period when the tax point occurs.

If the customer pays any remaining balance before the goods are delivered or the services are performed, another tax point is created when whichever of the following happens first:
- a VAT invoice is issued for the balance
- payment of the balance is received

The VAT on the balance must be included on the VAT Return for the period when the tax point occurs.

VAT does not have to be accounted for if a deposit is either:
- Refunded to the customer in full when they return goods safely, or
- Kept as compensation for loss of or damage to the goods.

Discounts on goods and services

If any goods or services supplied by a VAT-registered business are subject to a trade, bulk or other form of discount, VAT is charged on the VAT invoice on the discounted price rather than the full price.

Returned goods, credit notes, debit notes and VAT

For a buyer who has received a VAT invoice

If goods are returned to the seller for full or partial credit there are three options:
- return the invoice to the supplier and obtain a replacement invoice showing the proper amount of VAT due, if any
- obtain a credit note from the supplier
- issue a debit note to the supplier

If the buyer issues a debit note or receives a credit note, it must:
- record this in the accounting records
- enter it on the next VAT Return, deducting the VAT on the credit or debit note from the amount of VAT which can be reclaimed

For a seller who has issued a VAT invoice

If goods are returned by a customer, there are again three options:
- cancel and recover the original invoice, and issue a replacement showing the correct amount of any VAT due, if any
- issue a credit note to the customer
- obtain a debit note from the customer

If the seller issues a credit note or receives a debit note, it must:
- record this in the accounting records
- enter it on the next VAT Return, deducting the VAT on the credit or debit note from the amount of VAT payable

Entertainment expenses

Business entertainment

Business entertainment is any form of free or subsidised entertainment or hospitality to non-employees, for example suppliers and customers. Generally a business cannot reclaim input tax on business entertainment expenses. The exception is that input tax can be reclaimed in respect of entertaining overseas customers, but not UK or Isle of Man customers.

Employee expenses and entertainment

The business can, however, reclaim VAT on employee expenses and employee entertainment expenses if those expenses relate to travel and subsistence or where the entertainment applies only to employees.

When the entertainment is in respect of a mixed group of both employees and non-employees (eg customers and/or suppliers), the business can only reclaim VAT on the proportion of the expenses that is for employees and on the proportion for overseas customers.

Vehicles and motoring expenses

VAT and vehicles

When it buys a car a registered business generally cannot reclaim the VAT. There are some exceptions - for example, when the car is used mainly as one of the following:
- a taxi
- for driving instruction
- for self-drive hire

If the VAT on the original purchase price of a car bought new is not reclaimed, the business does not have to charge any VAT when it is sold. This is because the sale of the car is exempt for VAT purposes. If the business did reclaim the VAT when it bought the car new, VAT is chargeable when it comes to sell it.

VAT-registered businesses can generally reclaim the VAT when they buy a commercial vehicle such as a van, lorry or tractor.

Reclaiming VAT on road fuel

If the business pays for road fuel, it can deal with the VAT charged on the fuel in one of four ways:
- Reclaim all of the VAT. All of the fuel must be used only for business purposes.
- Reclaim all of the VAT and pay the appropriate fuel scale charge - this is a way of accounting for output tax on fuel that the business buys but that is then used for private motoring.
- Reclaim only the VAT that relates to fuel used for business mileage. Detailed records of business and private mileage must be kept.
- Do not reclaim any VAT. This can be a useful option if mileage is low and also if fuel is used for both business and private motoring. If the business chooses this option it must apply it to all vehicles, including commercial vehicles.

Transactions outside the UK

Exports, despatches and supplying goods abroad: charging VAT

If a business sells, supplies or transfers goods out of the UK to someone in another country it may need to charge VAT on them.

VAT on exports of goods to non-EU countries
Generally speaking, the business can zero-rate supplies exported outside the EU, provided it follows strict rules, obtains and keeps the necessary evidence, and obeys all laws.

The term 'exports' is reserved to describe sales to a country outside the EU. Goods supplied to another EU member state are technically known as despatches rather than exports.

VAT on despatches of goods to someone who is not VAT registered in another EU member state

When a business supplies goods to someone in another EU member state, and they are not registered for VAT in that country, it should normally charge VAT.

VAT on despatches of goods to someone who is VAT registered in another EU member state

If, however, goods are supplied to someone who is registered for VAT in the destination EU member state, the business can zero-rate the supply for VAT purposes, provided it meets certain conditions.

Imports, acquisitions and purchasing goods from abroad: paying and reclaiming VAT

Generally speaking, VAT is payable on all purchases of goods that are bought from abroad at the same rate that would apply to the goods if bought in the UK. The business must tell HMRC about goods that it imports, and pay any VAT and duty that is due.

VAT on imports of goods from non-EU countries

VAT may be charged on imports of goods bought from non-EU countries. The business can reclaim any VAT paid on the goods imported as input tax.

VAT on goods acquired from EU member states

If a business is registered for VAT in the UK and buys goods from inside the EU, these are known as acquisitions rather than imports. Usually no VAT is charged by the supplier but acquisition tax, at the same rate of VAT that would apply if the goods were supplied in the UK, is due on the acquisition. This is included in Box 2 of the VAT return. It can be reclaimed as input tax in Box 4 of the VAT return as if the goods were bought in the UK.

Bad debts

When a business can reclaim VAT on bad debts

VAT that has been paid to HMRC and which has not been received from the customer can be reclaimed as bad debt relief. The conditions are that:

- the debt is more than six months and less than four years and six months old
- the debt has been written off in the VAT account and transferred to a separate bad debt account
- the debt has not been sold or handed to a factoring company
- the business did not charge more than the normal selling price for the items

Bad debt relief does not apply when the cash accounting scheme is used because the VAT is not paid to HMRC until after the customer has paid it to the supplier.

How to claim bad debt relief

If the business is entitled to claim bad debt relief, add the amount of VAT to be reclaimed to the amount of VAT being reclaimed on purchases (input tax) and put the total figure in Box 4 of the VAT Return.

Effect of a change in the business

If a business closes down, relief for all outstanding bad debts up to and including the date of closure will need to be claimed, if eligible.

Where a business is acquired as a going concern and the acquiring business takes on the VAT registration of the closing business, it may be possible to transfer the outstanding bad debts from the old to the new business.

Completing the online VAT Return, box by box

The online VAT Return is completed as follows:

Box 1 – VAT due in this period on sales and other outputs

- This is the total amount of VAT charged on sales to customers. It also has to include VAT due to HMRC for other reasons, for example fuel scale charges.
- Include VAT due on a supply of services from another member state of the EC, where the supplier has "zero-rated" the supply.

Box 2 – VAT due in this period on acquisitions from other EC Member States

- VAT due, but not yet paid, on goods bought from other EU member states, and any services directly related to those goods (such as delivery charges). The business may be able to reclaim this amount, and if so it must be included in the total in Box 4.

Box 3 – Total VAT due (the sum of boxes 1 and 2). This is calculated automatically by the online return

Box 4 – VAT reclaimed in this period on purchases and other inputs (including acquisitions from the EC)

- This is the VAT charged on purchases for use in the business. It should also include:
  - VAT paid on imports from countries outside the EC
  - VAT due (but not yet paid) on goods from other EC member states, and any services directly related to those goods (such as delivery charges) - this is the figure in Box 2.
  - VAT due on a supply of services from a supplier in another member state of the EC where that supply has been "zero-rated" by the supplier. This will be the same amount as entered in Box 1 in respect of the same transaction.

Box 5 – Net VAT to be paid to HM Revenue & Customs or reclaimed by you (Difference between boxes 3 and 4). This is calculated automatically by the online return

Box 6 – Total value of sales and all other outputs excluding any VAT. Include your box 8 figure.

- Enter the total figure for sales (excluding VAT) for the period, that is the sales on which the VAT entered in Box 1 was based. Additionally, also include:
  - any zero-rated and exempt sales or other supplies made
  - any amount entered in Box 8
  - exports to outside the EC.

  The net amount of any credit notes issued, or debit notes received, is deducted.

Box 7 – Total value of purchases and all other inputs excluding any VAT. Include your box 9 figure.

- Enter the total figure for purchases (excluding VAT) for the period, that is the purchases on which the VAT entered in Box 4 was based. Additionally, also include:
  - any zero-rated and exempt purchases
  - any amount entered in Box 9
  - imports from outside the EU.

Box 8 – Total value of all supplies of goods and related costs, excluding any VAT, to other EC Member States.

- Enter the total value of goods supplied to another EC member state and services related to those goods (such as delivery charges).

Box 9 – Total value of all acquisitions of goods and related costs, excluding any VAT, from other EC Member States.

- Enter the total value of goods received from VAT registered suppliers in another EC member state and services related to those goods (such as delivery charges).

VAT periods, submitting returns and paying VAT

VAT Returns for transactions to the end of the relevant VAT period must be submitted by the due date shown on the VAT Return. VAT due must also be paid by the due date.

What is a VAT period?

A VAT period is the period of time over which the business records VAT transactions in the VAT account for completion of the VAT Return. The VAT period is three months (a quarter) unless the annual accounting scheme is used. The end dates of a business's four VAT periods are determined when it first registers for VAT, but it can choose to amend the dates on which its VAT periods end. This is often done to match VAT periods to accounting period ends.

Submitting VAT Returns online and paying HMRC electronically

It is mandatory for virtually all VAT-registered traders to submit their VAT Returns to HMRC using online filing, and to pay HMRC electronically.

Due dates for submitting the VAT Return and paying electronically

Businesses are responsible for calculating how much VAT they owe and for paying VAT so that the amount clears to HMRC's bank account on or before the due date. Paying on time avoids having to pay a surcharge for late payment.

The normal due date for submitting each VAT Return and electronically paying HMRC any VAT that is owed is one calendar month after the end of the relevant VAT period, unless the annual accounting scheme is operated. The normal due date for the return and payment can be found on the return.

Online filing and electronic payment mean that businesses get an extended due date for filing the return of seven extra calendar days after the normal due date shown on the VAT Return. This extra seven days also applies to paying HMRC so that the amount has cleared into HMRC's bank account. However this does not apply if the business uses the Annual Accounting Scheme for VAT.

If the business pays HMRC by Direct Debit, HMRC automatically collects payment from the business's bank account three bank working days after the extra seven calendar days following the normal due date.

If the business fails to pay cleared funds into HMRC's bank account by the payment deadline, or fails to have sufficient funds in its account to meet the direct debit, it may be liable to a surcharge for late payment.

Repayment of VAT

If the amount of VAT reclaimed (entered in Box 4) is more than the VAT to be paid (entered in Box 3), then the net VAT value in Box 5 is a repayment due to the business from HMRC.

HMRC is obliged to schedule this sum for repayment automatically, provided checks applied to the VAT Return do not indicate that such a repayment might not be due. There may be circumstances when the business does not receive the repayment automatically, for instance if there is an outstanding debt owed to HMRC.

Special accounting schemes

Annual Accounting Scheme for VAT

Using standard VAT accounting, four VAT Returns each year are required. Any VAT due is payable quarterly, and any VAT refunds due are also receivable quarterly.

Using the normal annual accounting scheme, the business makes nine interim payments at monthly intervals. There is only one VAT Return to complete, at the end of the year, when either a balancing payment is payable or a balancing refund is receivable.

Businesses can start on the annual accounting scheme if their estimated taxable turnover during the next tax year is not more than £1.35 million. Businesses already using the annual accounting scheme can continue to do so until the estimated taxable turnover for the next tax year exceeds £1.6 million. If the business is taken over as a going concern the acquiring business must assess the use of the annual accounting scheme in the context of the expected and combined turnover of the new business, and must immediately cease using the scheme if that is expected to exceed £1.6m.

Whilst using the annual accounting scheme the business may also be able to use either the cash accounting scheme or the flat rate scheme, but not both.

Benefits of annual accounting

- One VAT Return per year, instead of four.
- Two months after the tax period end to complete and send in the annual VAT Return and pay the balance of VAT payable, rather than the usual one month.
- Better management of cash flow by paying a fixed amount in nine instalments.
- Ability to make additional payments as and when required.
- Join from VAT registration day, or at any other time if already registered for VAT.

Disadvantages of annual accounting

- Only one repayment per year, which is not beneficial if the business regularly requires refunds.
- If turnover decreases, interim payments may be higher than the VAT payments would be under standard VAT accounting – again there is a need to wait until the end of the year to receive a refund.

Cash Accounting Scheme for VAT

Using standard VAT accounting, VAT is paid on sales within a VAT period whether or not the customer has paid. VAT is reclaimed on purchases whether or not the business has paid the supplier.

Using cash accounting, VAT is not paid until the customer has paid the invoice. If a customer never pays, the business never has to pay the VAT. VAT is reclaimed on purchases only when the business has paid the invoice.

Cash accounting can be used if the estimated taxable turnover during the next tax year is not more than £1.35 million. A business can continue to use cash accounting until its taxable turnover exceeds £1.6 million.

The cash accounting scheme may be used in conjunction with the annual accounting scheme but not with the flat rate scheme. If the business is taken over as a going concern the acquiring business must assess the use of the cash accounting scheme in the context of the expected and combined turnover of the new business, and must immediately cease using the scheme if that is expected to exceed £1.6m.

Benefits of cash accounting

Using cash accounting may help cash flow, especially if customers are slow payers. Payment of VAT is not made until the business has received payment from the customer, so if a customer never pays, VAT does not have to be paid on that bad debt as long as the business is using the cash accounting scheme.

Disadvantages of cash accounting

Using cash accounting may adversely affect cash flow:
*   The business cannot reclaim VAT on purchases until it has paid for them. This can be a disadvantage if most goods and services are purchased on credit.
*   Businesses which regularly reclaim more VAT than they pay will usually receive repayment later under cash accounting than under standard VAT accounting, unless they pay for everything at the time of purchase.
*   If a business starts using cash accounting when it starts trading, it will not be able to reclaim VAT on most start-up expenditure, such as initial stock, tools or machinery, until it has actually paid for those items.
*   When it leaves the cash accounting scheme the business will have to account for all outstanding VAT due, including on any bad debts.

Flat Rate Scheme for VAT

If its VAT-exclusive taxable turnover is less than £150,000 per year, the business could simplify its VAT accounting by registering on the Flat Rate Scheme and calculating VAT payments as a percentage of its total VAT-inclusive turnover. There is no reclaim of VAT on purchases - this is taken into account in calculating the flat rate percentage that applies to the business.

The VAT flat rate the business uses usually depends on its business type. It may pay a different rate if it only spends a small amount on goods.

Limited cost business

The business is classed as a 'limited cost business' if its goods cost less than either:
*   2% of its turnover
*   £1,000 a year (if its costs are more than 2%)

This means the business pays a flat rate of 16.5%, whatever its business type.

Non-limited cost businesses use their business type to determine the applicable flat rate.

Reclaim of VAT on capital expenditure goods

If the business uses the Flat Rate Scheme, it can reclaim the VAT it has been charged on a single purchase of capital expenditure goods where the amount of the purchase, including VAT, is £2,000 or more.

These capital expenditure goods are dealt with outside the Flat Rate Scheme. This means that the input tax is claimed in box 4 of the VAT return. If the supply is:
*   more than one purchase
*   under £2,000 including VAT, or

- of services

then no VAT is claimable, as this input tax is already taken into account in the calculation of the flat rate percentage.

The flat rate scheme can reduce the time needed in accounting for and working out VAT. Even though the business still needs to show a VAT amount on each VAT invoice issued, it does not need to record how much VAT it charged on every sale in its ledger accounts. Nor does it need to record the VAT paid on every purchase.

Once on the scheme, the business can continue to use it until its total business income exceeds £230,000. If the business is taken over as a going concern the acquiring business must assess the use of the flat rate scheme in the context of the expected and combined turnover of the new business, and must immediately cease using the scheme if that is expected to exceed £230,000. The flat rate scheme may be used in conjunction with the annual accounting scheme but not the cash accounting scheme.

Benefits of using the flat rate scheme

Using the flat rate scheme can save time and smooth cash flow. It offers these benefits:
- No need to record the VAT charged on every sale and purchase, as with standard VAT accounting. This can save time. But although the business only has to pay HMRC a percentage of its turnover, it must still show VAT at the appropriate normal rate (standard, reduced or zero) on the VAT invoices it issues.
- A first year discount. A business in its first year of VAT registration gets a 1% reduction in the applicable flat rate percentage until the day before the first anniversary of VAT registration.
- Fewer rules to follow, for instance no longer having to work out what VAT on purchases can or cannot be reclaimed.
- Peace of mind, less chance of mistakes and fewer worries about getting the VAT right.
- Certainty. The business always knows what percentage of takings has to be paid to HMRC.

Potential disadvantages of using the flat rate scheme

The flat rate percentages are calculated in a way that takes into account zero-rated and exempt sales. They also contain an allowance for the VAT spent on purchases. So the VAT Flat Rate Scheme might not be right for the business if:
- it buys mostly standard-rated items, as there is no reclaim of any VAT on purchases
- it regularly receives a VAT repayment under standard VAT accounting
- it makes a lot of zero-rated or exempt sales.
- It is a 'limited cost business'

Errors in previous VAT Returns

Action to be taken at the end of the VAT period

At the end of the VAT period, the business should calculate the net value of all the errors and omissions found during the period that relate to VAT Returns already submitted - that is, any tax which should have been claimed back is subtracted from any additional tax due to HMRC, and any tax that should have been paid is added. Any deliberate errors must not be included - these must be separately declared to HMRC.

What the business should do next depends on whether the net value of all the errors is less than or greater than the 'error correction reporting threshold', which is the greater of:
- £10,000
- 1% of the box 6 figure on the VAT Return for the period when the error was discovered - subject to an upper limit of £50,000

If the net value of all the errors is less than the error reporting threshold then, if preferred, the errors may be corrected by making an adjustment on the current VAT Return (Method 1).

However, if the value of the net VAT error discovered is above this threshold, it must be declared to HMRC separately, in writing (Method 2).

How to adjust the VAT Return: Method 1

Errors from previous VAT Returns can be corrected by adjusting the VAT amounts on the current VAT Return.

At the end of the VAT period when the errors are discovered, the VAT account of output tax due or input tax claimed is adjusted by the net amount of all errors. The VAT account must show the amount of the adjustment being made to the VAT Return.

If more than one error is discovered in the same exercise, the net value of all the errors is used to adjust the VAT liability on the VAT Return.

Either Box 1 or Box 4 is adjusted, as appropriate. For example, if the business discovers that it did not account for VAT payable to HMRC of £100 on a supply made in the past, and also did not account for £60 VAT reclaimable on a purchase, it should add £40 to the Box 1 figure on the current VAT Return.

How to separately declare an error to HMRC: Method 2

For certain errors a separate declaration is required to the relevant HMRC VAT Error Correction Team in writing about the mistake. The simplest way to tell them is to use Form VAT 652 "Notification of Errors in VAT Returns", which is for reporting errors on previous returns, but the business does not have to use Form VAT 652 - it can simply write a letter instead.

Businesses may, if they wish, use this method for errors of any size, even those which are below the error reporting threshold i.e. instead of a Method 1 error correction. Using this method means the business must not make adjustment for the same errors on a later VAT Return.

Method 2 must always be used if the net error exceeds the error reporting threshold or if the errors made on previous returns were made deliberately.

Surcharges, penalties and assessments

Surcharges for missed VAT Return or VAT payment deadlines

VAT-registered businesses must submit a VAT Return and pay any VAT by the relevant due date. If HMRC receives a return or VAT payment after the due date, the business is 'in default' and may have to pay a surcharge in addition to the VAT that is owed.

The first default is dealt with by a warning known as a 'Surcharge Liability Notice'. This notice tells the business that if it submits or pays late ('defaults') again during the following 12 months - known as the surcharge period - it may be charged a surcharge.

Submitting or paying late again during the surcharge period could result in a 'default surcharge'. This is a percentage of any unpaid VAT owed. Where a correct return is not submitted at all, HMRC will estimate the amount of VAT owed and base the surcharge on that amount (this is known as an assessment – see below).

HMRC assessments

Businesses have a legal obligation to submit VAT Returns and pay any VAT owed to HMRC by the relevant due date. If they do not submit a return, HMRC can issue an assessment which shows the amount of VAT that HMRC believes it is owed, based on HMRC's best estimate.

Penalties for careless and deliberate errors

Careless and deliberate errors will be liable to a penalty, whether they are adjusted on the VAT Return or separately declared.

If a business discovers an error which is neither careless nor deliberate, HMRC expects that it will take steps to adjust or declare it, as appropriate. If the business fails to take such steps, the inaccuracy will be treated as careless and a penalty will be due.

Penalties for inaccurate returns

Penalties may be applied if a VAT Return is inaccurate, and correcting this means tax is unpaid, understated, over-claimed or under-assessed. Telling HMRC about inaccuracies as soon as the business is aware of them may reduce any penalty that is due, in some cases to zero.

Penalty for late registration

Failure to register for VAT with HMRC at the right time may make a business liable to a late registration penalty.

Penalty for failure to disclose business changes

A business which undergoes a change which either cancels the existing registration or otherwise alters the registration details will face a civil penalty if it fails to disclose the changes to HMRC within 30 days of the change.

Finding out more information about VAT

Most questions can be answered by referring to the VAT section of the HMRC website.

VAT Enquiries Helpline

If the answer to a question is not on the HMRC website, the quickest and easiest way is to ring the VAT Enquiries Helpline where most VAT questions can be answered.

Letters to HMRC

The VAT General Enquiries helpline can answer most questions relating to VAT, but there may be times when it is more appropriate to write to HMRC.

This would apply if:
- the VAT information published by HMRC - either on the website or in printed notices and information sheets - has not answered a question
- the VAT General Enquiries helpline has advised the business to write
- there is real doubt about how VAT affects a particular transaction, personal situation or business

If HMRC already publishes information that answers the question, their response will give the relevant details.

Visits by VAT officers

On a control visit to a business a VAT officer can examine VAT records to make sure that they are up to date. They also check that amounts claimed from or paid to the government are correct.

for your notes

for your notes

for your notes

for your notes